Thomas Adès in Five Essays

Thomas Adès in Five Essays

Drew Massey

OXFORD
UNIVERSITY PRESS

OXFORD
UNIVERSITY PRESS

Oxford University Press is a department of the University of Oxford. It furthers
the University's objective of excellence in research, scholarship, and education
by publishing worldwide. Oxford is a registered trade mark of Oxford University
Press in the UK and certain other countries.

Published in the United States of America by Oxford University Press
198 Madison Avenue, New York, NY 10016, United States of America.

Library of Congress Cataloging-in-Publication Data
Names: Massey, Drew (Drew Michael) author.
Title: Thomas Adès in five essays / Drew Massey.
Description: New York : Oxford University Press, 2020. | Includes index.
Identifiers: LCCN 2020018290 (print) | LCCN 2020018291 (ebook) |
ISBN 9780199374960 (hardback) | ISBN 9780197540381 (epub) | ISBN 9780197540398
Subjects: LCSH: Adès, Thomas—Criticism and interpretation.
Classification: LCC ML410.A2337 M37 2020 (print) |
LCC ML410.A2337 (ebook) | DDC 780.92—dc23
LC record available at https://lccn.loc.gov/2020018290
LC ebook record available at https://lccn.loc.gov/2020018291

3 5 7 9 8 6 4 2

Printed by Sheridan Books, Inc., United States of America

Contents

Acknowledgments

Many people provided feedback about this project during its gestation over the last decade; I'd like in particular to thank Ryan Bañagale and Philip Gentry for some critical early support as I was writing the first chapters and the book proposal. My colleagues and friends at Binghamton University—especially Dan Davis and John Havard—were fantastic sounding boards as I tried on various ideas. As were my students there. The extended family of Adès scholars is a welcoming and convivial crew; I especially benefitted in my conversations with Ed Venn, Phil Rupprecht, John Roeder, and Emma Gallon. Ed and Phil in particular provided valuable feedback about the manuscript as a whole as I neared the end of the writing process; so did Jeff Means, Matthew Somoroff, and Robert Boyers. I am grateful for these labors of love.

Aspects of this research were supported by grants from Binghamton University and its Institute for Advanced Studies in the Humanities, as well as and the National Endowment for the Humanities. Suzanne Ryan and Norm Hirschy, my editors at Oxford, were masterful in shepherding the project to its completion. I'm also grateful to Sally Cavender and her colleagues at Faber for their valuable assistance in licensing the musical examples. Speaking of musical examples, I'd like to thank Martyn Burns, Karl Enton, Bryan Junod, Scott Lee, and Christian Marten for their expertise in typesetting the musical examples.

This book also reflects my perspective insofar as I have come to know Adès and his partner Fil Jones as friends over the years I have spent writing, seeing them socially both in the US and abroad throughout the latter part of the writing process. My friendship with them has been a great personal delight of the last several years, and while those relationships inevitably inform what follows, this is a book that remains centered on Adès's achievements as a musician.

I am particularly indebted to Tony Fogg and Paul Buttenwieser for arranging introductions when Adès and I were still relative strangers.

Finally, thanks to my husband Gabe, who was with me through this whole process and cheered me on through its fits and starts. I would never have made it without him.

Introduction

The Informal Adès

Instability is a recurring theme in Thomas Adès's book of interviews, *Full of Noises*. Adès declares on the book's second page: "Where there is life . . . there is no stability."[1] Adès continues, however, by executing what proves to be only the first of several U-turns in the book: "a lot of musical material—maybe all—tends to desire stability or resolution of some kind, unless it's held in a kind of equilibrium, which is still a volatile situation. That's the way I understand everything in . . . musical history. The music we listen to is the residue of an endless search for stability."[2] I would continue Adès's observation by noting that the music he has composed enacts this restless quest through its kaleidoscopic contexts and incompatibilities. It is virtually impossible to succinctly describe Adès's sound world because it is so expansive. In *The Lover in Winter* we encounter an arctic austerity possible only by means of the Latin setting for countertenor; we hear the sheer camp exuberance of *Powder Her Face*; in *Asyla*, we move from the mysterious opening to the ecstatic "rave" movement in the course of a dozen minutes; elsewhere we encounter an almost crystalline formalism, as in *Polaris*. Any representative cross section of his compositions would reveal similar striations of apparently contradictory or incompatible musical thought. Though he is unmistakably a rigorous formalist composer, his work is also notable for its referential character, for its opulence and its improbable combination of delirium and refinement. In denying us any sense of stability he simultaneously enchants us, and that is why I decided to write this book.

The volume you are holding now is an introduction to those who are curious about but unfamiliar with recurring themes in Adès's music, from the beginning of his career in 1989 until his 2016 opera *The Exterminating Angel*; it is an epistle to my colleagues who have engaged in scholarly study of Adès; it is an appreciation for readers who are already familiar with Adès's work. This book is not "balanced"—or, should I say, "stable"—in terms of its consideration of Adès's music: his piano piece *Traced Overhead* hardly makes an appearance, and his landmark *Asyla* is considered mostly in passing. I have spent considerable time, by contrast, contemplating the significance of his

Thomas Adès in Five Essays. Drew Massey, Oxford University Press (2021). © Oxford University Press.
DOI: 10.1093/oso/9780199374960.001.0001.

arrangements of both his own works and the works of others. These decisions have been made largely because of my personal reactions to Adès's music, though some of them are grounded in the broader scholarly frame in which this book exists. For example, Ed Venn has written an entire book on *Asyla*, and I refer the reader to his scholarship—and the work of many others—throughout the course of this study.

I take what I call, for lack of a better term, an "informal" approach, not only because it suits my own temperament, but also because it suits the sensibility of the composer who is my subject. I use *informality* here in the everyday sense of the word, but also in a more specific sense: the sense that Adès is a composer who deserves as nimble a consideration as I may hope to provide, because his own approach to creating music has consistently involved a process of aesthetic discovery that resists a single thoroughgoing analytical or conceptual lens.

This conventional notion of informality is easy enough to understand; I am borrowing the second sense of the word from Theodor Adorno and his 1961 essay "Vers une musique informelle." Adorno is hardly an obvious place to go looking for a better vantage point for Adès's music. Adorno decries fetishism; Adès finds what he calls "fetish notes" underappreciated. Adorno is overwhelmingly concerned with Schoenberg and Webern in his essay; Adès's affinities with Berg are more palpable than with those others in the Second Viennese School. Adorno was famously hostile to the culture industry; Adès is a voracious enthusiast for music, art, and literature that strikes his fancy, no matter what its source or popular appeal might be. Moreover, "Vers une musique informelle" lies somewhat outside of the center of Adorno's philosophical preoccupations and is a late essay that has received relatively little attention from scholars and critics.[3] It was written from Adorno's vantage point as an éminence grise at Darmstadt, where the consequences of postwar formalism were starting to seem to Adorno like an aesthetic cul-de-sac. Hence the first, most general point of connection is to note that Adès came of age in an era of seeming dead ends, as well: the diverse practices lumped together under postmodernism seemed to have a limited future after the fall of the Berlin wall in 1989 (the year of Adès's first published composition), and the quest for a vocabulary that would describe overarching cultural forces after the heyday of postmodernism has become something of a cottage industry since 9/11.

Adorno proposed the ideal of an "informal" music because he felt that both neoclassicism and total serialism had no real future on account of their ideological rigidity. He tells us at the beginning of the essay that his subject matter will be slippery: "*Musique informelle* resists definition in the botanical terms of the positivisits. If there is a tendency, an actual trend, which the word serves to bring into focus, it is one which mocks all efforts at definition." Without saying exactly what it is, Adorno "stake[s] out the parameters" of a *musique informelle*: it is

> a type of music which has discarded all forms which are external or abstract or which confront it in an inflexible way. At the same time, although such music should be completely free of anything irreducibly alien to itself or superimposed on it, it should nevertheless constitute itself in an objectively compelling way, in the musical substance itself, and not in terms of external laws.[4]

In Adorno's mind, music that has achieved this ideal will be more fully alive, animated from within by the intentional interventions of the composer.[5] Adorno's path forward (toward, let's not forget, a horizon, rather than a specific practice), relied on a recuperation of musical subjectivity into contemporary practice that he felt had become preoccupied with objectivity in different guises. There is no room in Adorno's utopia for the abdication of intentionality (Boulez, Cage) or for historicist forms embraced for their perceived objectivity (Stravinsky).

This is the second point of connection between Adorno's imagined future and Adès's path as a composer. Adorno's *musique informelle* at the very least asks us not to compartmentalize two of the most important dimensions of Adès's work: first, his retrospective gaze and apparently endless appetite for allusion and the play of musical surfaces, and second, his formidable technical capability. These two trends are mutually ensnared for Adès; consider how admiringly he speaks of Berg's *Lulu* as a work in which "the formal processes are so overgrown that they cease to advertise themselves."[6] Furthermore, if we take seriously Adorno's vision of a music that has "discarded all forms which are external or abstract," we might start to view apparently contradictory dimensions of Adès's work as emanating from a common font. For example, Adès has consistently insisted on the sovereignty of musical material—"notes want certain things," in his own formulation. At the same time, he is a composer who has become known for his fascination with surface elements that signal their meanings through the shared convention of musical styles—consider for example his prominent use of various dance forms in *Totentanz*. From one perspective the ostensible inevitability lurking behind "notes wanting certain things" may seem to be at cross-purposes with the imperatives of composing in a particular vernacular or genre. I would argue, however, that these apparent contradictions are merely distinct impulses in a larger equation that keeps subjective and objective dimensions in a tense dialectic.

For Adorno, *musique informelle* emanates from a shifting balance between material, composition, and idiom, and this is an instructive dynamic for considering Adès. The layers of accumulated signification in a work like *In Seven Days*, for example, go hand in hand with extremely strict formal processes, contributing to the work's seemingly infinite "spiral" of material, as Adès calls it. The third movement of *In Seven Days*, with its elaborate serial processes, which themselves are contained within a variation form in a programmatic context, provides just one example of the *informelle* in practice. What was once seen as the absence of intentional sculpting of the music for Adorno (a rigid serial process, eliminating subjectivity) becomes rather an idiom for Adès, a means to mediate between the transcendent and the immanent. Subjectivity and idiom are bound up in other ways in *In Seven Days*. Adès tells us that the piano part is also symbolic of human consciousness, serving to explain its hulking presence in the sixth movement. We will return to *In Seven Days* in due course; the point to note now is that this work illuminates one of the ways that Adès's music mediates between subjective and objective modes of signification.

It makes sense to be informal toward Adorno's *musique informelle*: anyone with a passing familiarity with Adès's compositions would see the folly of pursuing Adorno's notion of an informal music as a single explanatory lens for Adès's work. One limitation of Adorno's *musique informelle* is its hermeticism. Opera hardly makes an appearance in Adorno's essay; Adès's three operas lay at the heart of his output. Furthermore, Adorno's theory does not engage with an important feature of Adès's work: its so-called "pseudomorphism," or the quality of his music that draws on metaphors from the visual and narrative arts.[7] If some of Adès's worldview is elucidated by Adorno's utopian ruminations about a music whose exquisitely calibrated consequentiality gives rise to perfectly liberated musical experiences, there are also qualities of Adès's work which reveal an exuberant embrace of the world and a constant move between the formalistic and the referential. It is this very oscillation that is the center of the idea of metamodernism, a conceptual framework that has received its most thorough exposition in Timotheus Vermeulen's and Robin van den Akker's 2010 essay "Notes on Metamodernism."[8] Metamodernism is, like *musique informelle*, a somewhat obscure way of looking at recent composition and artwork. I have selected it not for its notoriety, but rather for its way of opening a potentially rich vein of inquiry. Metamodernism, like Adorno's essay, is a trailhead, not a map.[9]

Vermeulen and Van den Akker have explored the idea that visual artists, architects, and filmmakers are beginning to synthesize elements of postmodernism and modernism into works that reflect new "structures of feeling" that are peculiar to the twenty-first century.[10] Vermeulen and Van den Akker are not, strictly speaking, dialectical in their approach. There is no grand synthesis at the end of their analysis. Rather, metamodernist work, in their formulation, "oscillates between a modern enthusiasm and a postmodern irony, between hope and melancholy, between naïveté and knowingness, empathy and apathy, unity and plurality, totality and fragmentation, purity and ambiguity."[11] Metamodernism is not so much a set of practices as it is a sensibility, and the sheer diversity of Adès's output makes it at first glance a comfortable fit: consider the wildly different worlds of *Polaris*, the Piano Quintet, and *Life Story*.

Other commentators on Adès have described his music along similar lines. In a 1999 article about Adès, Richard Taruskin proposed that Adès had successfully managed to "buck sterile utopia while avoiding the opposing pitfall of ironic pastiche."[12] In a parallel vein, Venn singled out Arnold Whittall's notion of a "'continuing, intensifying dialogue' between opposing tendencies" as central to an understanding of Adès and other contemporary composers.[13] What all these writers would probably agree on when it comes to Adès is that the representational and the formal, the postmodern and the modern, the "dispersive" and the "unifying" (to borrow the art historian Molly Warnock's terms) seem to be mutually constitutive in many of his compositions.[14] And while Vermeulen and Van den Akker may overstate the case for the absolute novelty of metamodernism's structures of feeling in the twenty-first century— visual artists like Jean Arp, Simon Hantaï, and Sigmar Polke were exploring similar oscillations decades before Adès, and Vermeulen and Van den Akker themselves discuss the performance art of Bas Jan Ader, who died in 1975— metamodernism nevertheless forms an approach to contemplating Adès which brings in to focus his contributions not only to contemporary composition but the broader contemporary art world.

I hope to persuade the reader by the end of this book that a so-called "informal" approach to Adès provides an understanding of him that we would otherwise lack. The importance of "influence" provides one clear consequence of such a worldview. Whittall has noted the "pleasure of allusion" in Adès's relationship to existing music, distinguishing this stance from Harold Bloom's more widely used (and abused) "anxiety of influence." Yet Adès offered his own peculiar view of influence in *Full of Noises* in a discussion of Stravinsky: "I'm fortunate in that I love everything he did and find so much to learn from. I think you will get further if you're learning from examples that you can't replicate that easily, that run counter to your own nature . . . Often with influences, one is a face at the window, looking in on something one wants." In contrast to what he calls the "volatility" of his own music, Adès explains, "part of the fascination for me of Stravinsky's writing is that it's almost as though his ink has a kind of built-in fixative. The moment the note hits the paper, bang, it sticks. Like a dart in a dartboard."[15] In other words, if we take Adès's comments at face value, influence in his mind is rather upside down: we should be looking for composers rather *unlike* Adès as potential loci for his personal influences. If we don't take Adès at face value (or, more precisely, characterize this upside-downness as just one impulse among many constituting his sonic world), we need not abandon the more obvious points of reference for his work. Even though Adès himself has resisted the comparison, I argue that his opera *The Tempest* is almost unavoidably in conversation with Britten's *A Midsummer Night's Dream*. In other words, influence in Adès's case might be seen as a negotiation of different models of the phenomenon, between anxiety and pleasure, between affinity and difference, between his notes and his words. Balancing all of the contrasting impulses is no easy historiographic task—and my views here are almost certain to require further qualification as Adès continues to compose. At the same time, I hope to offer some ways of understanding a few of the beguiling contradictions in Adès's music.

This book, like every book, is also a book about its author. I moved from a professorship at an American university to a career in the technology world over the course of writing these essays. As such, the ghosts of academic debates haunt these pages, while toward the end of the writing process (which is not to say toward the end of the book) I became more concerned about impressing upon the reader the broader cultural significance of Adès's music. Central to that significance are the contradictions that inform the composer's idiom and musical vision. In five essays that are more or less independent from one another I have sought to move between resolutely different modes of reading, some of the time "subjective" (or allusive, or extrageneric) and elsewhere "objective" (or analytical, or focused on "the notes themselves.") I begin with a consideration of Adès's compositions written in reference to a preexisting musical work, whether his own or by another composer—an allusive process if there ever was one. In the second chapter, I turn my attention toward a more strictly analytical practice by contemplating his ambivalent embrace of serialism. The last three chapters explore ways that Adès negotiates this divide between subject and object, first in *The Tempest*, then in Adès's so-called surrealist works, and finally in his larger works written between 2006 and 2016.

One challenge for anyone writing on Adès is to fully absorb the dialectical way that his mind works, as revealed in *Full of Noises* and in so many of his compositions. Adès seems happy to hold many apparently contradictory ideas in his head at once as he composes, and I don't see why we shouldn't do the same as we listen to his work. The present study, therefore, cannot truly begin until I have sounded my own note of instability. A historiography of Adès will necessarily be as tense and ambiguous as Adorno's *musique informelle* or Vermeulen and van den Akker's "metamodernism." But the inevitable frustrations that come with such an unsettled perspective are perhaps where the meaning ultimately lies. Commentators on Adès would do well to keep Adès's own maxim posted above their desk: "There is banality lurking in [all] directions."[16]

1
The Glossary

> It's completely pretentious to imagine that you can do without other music.
>
> —Thomas Adès

If Adès were strictly a composer, it would be easier to know where to begin. Because of his polymathy as not only a composer, but also a pianist, a conductor, and, sometimes, an author, however, our first stops are not his most well-known pieces, but rather a consideration of pieces based on the work of earlier composers. Adès's retrospective gaze and his multifaceted musicality are inextricably related, and these points of contact are clearly demonstrated in his works which respond to complete, preexisting musical pieces.[1] These efforts, which span his entire active career, are listed in Table 1.1. I refer to them collectively as Adès's "glossary," drawing upon that word's generally neutral form as a commentary, exposition, or clarification. At the same time, the word "gloss" can also indicate apparent superficiality (as in "to gloss over") or, more obscurely, a sophistic or disingenuous reading, and these less common connotations will also prove relevant to this exploration of Adès's music.

One might ask why the works listed here deserve special consideration. Adès's compositional language is marked by allusion, and his mastery in this regard has been explored by Arnold Whittall and others. A number of his compositions, such as *Sonata da Caccia* and his *Mazurkas*, are redolent of earlier styles and genres. I argue that Adès's glosses complement, but also stand in contrast to, less specifically intertextual moments in his music because of the clarity with which an existing work is transformed in his glossary. I might chuckle at the exaggerated use of chromatic thirds in Adès's *Brahms*, or enjoy a glimmer of recognition when I hear Mozart quoted in *Arcadiana*, but these examples are so different in degree from a full-blown arrangement that they constitute a different relationship between the original and Adès's creation.[2] When considered as a body of work on to itself, the glossary constitutes Adès's most direct confrontation with the musical past.

Thomas Adès in Five Essays. Drew Massey, Oxford University Press (2021). © Oxford University Press.
DOI: 10.1093/oso/9780199374960.001.0001.

Table 1.1 Thomas Adès's Glossary (1990–2016)

Title	Year	Instrumentation	Source	Described by Adès as a(n):
Darknesse Visible	1992	Piano solo	Dowland, "In Darknesse Let Mee Dwell."	Explosion
Les Baricades Mistérieuses	1994	B-flat clarinet, B-flat bass clarinet, viola, cello, double bass	Couperin	Transcription
Cardiac Arrest	1995	B-flat clarinet, B-flat bass clarinet, viola, cello, double bass, piano duet	Madness	Arrangement
Study No. 6 & 7	1998	Two pianos	Nancarrow	Transcription
Scenes from the Tempest	2004	Large orchestra and singers	Adès, *The Tempest*	Concert setting
Court Studies	2005	Clarinet, piano, violin, cello	Adès, *The Tempest*	Derivation
Three Studies from Couperin	2006	Alto flute, bass flute, B-flat clarinet, bassoon, French horns, trumpet, percussion, two string orchestras	Couperin, *Les Amusemens; Les Tours de Passe-Passe; L'Âme-en-Peine*	Studies
Dances from Powder Her Face	2007	Large orchestra	Adès	Concert setting
Concert Paraphrase on Powder Her Face	2009	Piano solo	Adès	Paraphrase
Two songs from The Tempest for Voice and Piano	2012	Countertenor and piano	Purcell, *The Tempest*	Arrangement
Intermezzo from The Tempest Suite for harp and piano	2012	Harp and piano	Sibelius	Arrangement

The works in the glossary do more than show Adès peering over his shoulder at what has come before. They also show Adès's sophistication as a performer, and in that respect lie at the nexus of his multiple careers, illuminating the divide between the conductor's podium, the piano bench, and the composer's studio that he has negotiated with remarkable finesse. As we will see, there are several different ways in which Adès allows for a certain conceptual slippage between executant, listener, and composer in these pieces. As David Trippett has noted in his scholarship on Liszt, such moments of slippage have occurred at other times and places, and have led scholars to ask, "Who is speaking?"[3] In the case of Adès, works such as *Darknesse Visible* and his transcriptions of Nancarrow's studies employ subtle notational riddles that also posit the question *Who is listening?* The answers to these questions are particular to the individual pieces, but when taken as a whole they show that Adès uses the occasion of arrangement to offer visions of pieces which reflect his fully integrated musical subjectivity. These answers appear in moments ranging from the deft distortions of *Darknesse Visible*, to the exacting exploration of Couperin's ornaments and phrases that animates *Three Studies from Couperin*, to the understated virtuosity of Adès's transcription of Nancarrow's sixth study for player piano.

Several subordinate themes are evident in the glossary as well, and hint at other interrelationships between performance and composition in Adès's mind. *Darknesse Visible*, for example, also traffics in a language of difference in which Adès maps his own distinctive path through the territory of an existing work, intensifying, elaborating, and reconfiguring the source material as he sees fit. In a different vein, Adès's glossary also reveals his fascination with machines and strict formal processes of all kinds. This trend is particularly apparent in moments depicting either the absence of the human or the presence of the mechanical in *Concert Paraphrase on "Powder Her Face"*, or in Adès's settings of Nancarrow's music for player piano, respectively. These pieces reflect Adès's broader interest in the mechanical and formalistic: there is the oft-mentioned mimicry of electronic dance music in his orchestral work *Asyla*; his Violin Concerto (to name just one example) features the occasional rhythmic canon; *The Four Quarters* opens with a striking juxtaposition of isorhythm and serialism.[4] The mechanical also exists as an independent thread in Adès's music: consider the programmatic elements of a work like *Living Toys*, which at one point depicts a child dreaming that he "is in a film, in deepest space, dismantling a great computer."[5]

Neither automatism nor alterity should be particularly surprising themes to tease out of Adès's glossary; the family of practices we might broadly describe as "arrangement" walk the narrow corridor framed by these two considerations. On the one hand, an arrangement creates an interpretive gap between the source and target, no matter how small, thereby opening a breach of difference where some meaning resides.[6] On the other hand, there is at least the nominal goal of preserving the essence of the original, however that essence may be construed, and hence de-emphasizing the agency of the glossator.[7] Put another way, as a whole the glossary reveals Adès as a man who carefully reads—and, crucially, performs—the past while defending the absolute inviolability of his aesthetic sensibility, and moreover shows him at his most insightfully ironic, polemically enigmatic, and sincerely enthusiastic.

Difference

Luciano Berio—a composer widely known for his own arrangements and use of existing music—has suggested that composition can constitute a kind of discussion of an existing work:

> I'd had it in mind for a long time to explore from the inside a piece of music from the past: a creative exploration that was at the same time an analysis, a commentary and an extension of the original. This follows from my principle that, for a composer, the best way to analyze and comment on a piece is to do something, using materials from that piece.[8]

He went on to offer one of his own examples of such a process, discussing a plan he had to "harmonically 'explode'" the last three movements of Beethoven's op. 131. In Berio's mind, the finished product of such a process centers on conveying his own thoughts on a piece, and offering his own perspective on a work's important features.

It is not clear whether it was a coincidence or a nod to Berio when Adès decided to describe his piano piece *Darknesse Visible* as an "explosion," but Adès's work sits comfortably as an "analysis, a commentary, and an extension" of its source. Adès offered his own description of the work on its title page:

> This piece is an explosion of John Dowland's lute song "In Darknesse Let Mee Dwell" (1610). No notes have been added; indeed, some have been removed. Patterns latent in the original have been isolated and regrouped, with the aim of illuminating the song from within, as if during the course of a performance.[9]

Adès's note suggests a number of priorities. First, he fastidiously avoids the words "transcription," "arrangement," or "paraphrase," instead offering the more unorthodox "explosion," suggesting that he will be significantly departing from Dowland's song. The second sentence of his description, however, indicates his fidelity to the original work. Table 1.2 shows how closely Adès's arrangement adheres to the overall plan of Dowland's song; there are neither significant interpolations nor cuts. Finally, in the third sentence he suggests that what he is offering is no mere copy, but rather a product that is similar to a performance. In other words, he seems to promise the listener something rather special, an experience of him "illuminating the work from within," as if we were sitting at the piano bench with Adès as he plays the piece and tours its nooks and crannies. This subtly didactic

Table 1.2 "In Darknesse Let Mee Dwell," Concordance with *Darknesse Visible*.

Dowland Song	Adès Bars
(Instrumental Introduction)	1–7
In darknesse let mee dwell,	8–13
the ground shall sorrow be,	14–18
The roofe Dispaire to barre	19–23
all cheerfull light from mee,	24–26
The wals of marble blacke	27–30
that moistened still shall weepe,	30–38
My musicke, hellish, jarring sounds	40–49
to banish friendly sleepe.	49–54
Thus wedded to my woes,	55–58
and bedded to my Tombe,	62–66
O let me living die,	67–73
till death doe come.	74–81
In darknesse let mee dwell.	84–88

element of *Darknesse Visible* is further underscored by its status as Adès's only work which features a multicolored score. At the same time, the colored score would only be meaningful to a performer (or a listener armed with a score), and so Adès's likening *Darknesse Visible* to a kind of performance of Dowland requires a certain conceptual overlap, on Adès's part, between pianist and audience. Put another way, the pianist *is* the audience for certain aspects of *Darknesse Visible*. This is only the first example we will encounter of Adès treating text and act coterminously, and is emblematic of a larger trend in the glossary, wherein his arrangements take on a conspicuously performative dimension of their own.

Despite the multicolored score, Adès is careful not to overstate its significance, writing in a performance note: "Colours are used purely to differentiate between individual voices and their various distinct timbres during a given passage. The colours have no especial analytical or structural significance with regard to the piece as a whole."[10] The multiple colors of the vocal lines seem to deliberately mislead the player at a few points, when Dowland's tune moves from one voice to another (Example 1.1). In this example, one of the middle voices is an amalgam of Dowland's melody and bass, and Adès smoothly pivots from one to the next. Here again, Adès's setting slyly lodges a problem for both the performer and listener. If one is unfamiliar with "In Darknesse Let Mee Dwell," the moment seems unremarkable. If one does know Dowland's song, it creates an unsettling sense of discontinuity.

Example 1.1

a) Dowland, "In Darknesse Let Mee Dwell," excerpt. Number next to notes indicate concordance.

b) Adès, *Darknesse Visible*, mm. 30–35. © 1998 Faber Music Ltd, reproduced by kind permission of the publishers.

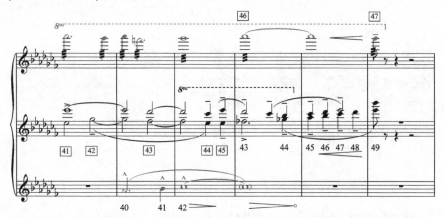

Adès's comment that "no notes have been added; indeed, some have been removed" understates the transformation of his work, since he suspends or adjusts harmonic implications throughout the piece, providing an overall effect of a work which is slightly unmoored from its A-flat minor tonality. Although all of the lines of Dowland's song are recognizable, Adès also provides numerous supplemental lines that are part of Dowland's lute tablature for the work.[11] But the notes that are removed are equally important: at several points Adès has omitted passages from the bass which would offer a strong cadential implication (Example 1.2). For example, at the beginning of *Darknesse Visible*, Adès fragments the falling fifth from E-flat to A-flat, which Dowland uses to signal the entrance of the vocal line. While Adès retains a strongly articulated movement from G-natural to A-flat in the upper register of the piano at the corresponding point in m. 8, the motion feels like a less explicit arrival than Dowland's gesture. Similarly, Adès does not allow the end of Dowland's fourth line of text to find harmonic purchase in mm. 25, by introducing a bass line which clouds the cadential implications present in Dowland's original. Finally, in m. 81, which corresponds to the conclusive penultimate cadence in

Example 1.2 Evaded or weakened cadences in *Darknesse Visible*.

Dowland's song, Adès disrupts the texture with a forceful F-flat, implying a deceptive cadence, and offering one final stubborn refusal to live up to harmonic expectations.

The main "explosive" technique Adès uses in *Darknesse Visible*, which serves to obscure Dowland's original in its own way, is extended octave displacement of Dowland's material. Adès first uses this technique when setting the second line of text, "the ground shall sorrow be" (Example 1.3). As the rhythmic density of the original accelerates, the octave displacement in *Darknesse Visible* increases. Here, Adès's setting of Dowland's melody begins in the upper reaches of the piano, and swoops down dramatically, while a slightly modified version of the accompaniment encompasses a similarly broad sweep of the keyboard in the opposite direction.

Another "explosive" effect, in addition to the octave displacement, is Adès's exaggerated use of rhythmic augmentation and diminution. Most of Adès's work quotes Dowland's tune at half-speed: a half note in Dowland becomes a whole note in *Darknesse Visible*. But at the most dramatically tense moment of the original song, corresponding to the text "let me living die," Adès's arrangement tilts radically in the other direction, setting Dowland's sixteenth notes as thirty-second notes, swerving to a diminution by half of the original quotation, and diminution by a quarter of the overall scheme of *Darknesse Visible* (Example 1.4). This passage also

Example 1.3

a) Dowland, "In Darknesse Let Mee Dwell," excerpt.

b) Adès, *Darknesse Visible*, mm. 14–18.

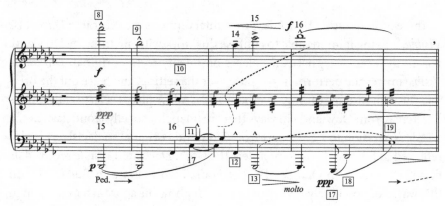

Example 1.4

a) Dowland, "In Darknesse Let Mee Dwell," excerpt.

b) Adès, *Darknesse Visible*, mm. 67–72.

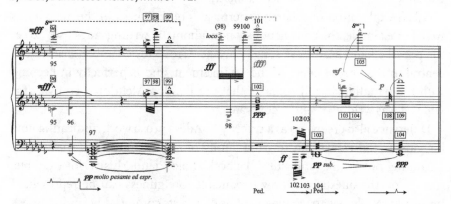

features the first point where notes are doubled in octaves, reinforcing the dramatic arrival of the narrator's anguished plea. At another point, Adès strikes two notes of Dowland's melody simultaneously, creating a jarring minor second (Example 1.5).

Example 1.5 Adès, *Darknesse Visible*, mm. 61–62.

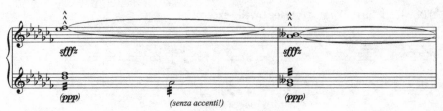

There is no question that Adès's own interventions are central to *Darknesse Visible*, making it impossible to confuse this work with anything by Dowland. For all the emphasis that Adès places on fidelity to the original, *Darknesse Visible* invites the performer to puzzle over the setting, and tease out the original through careful reading. In other words, Adès's piece seeks to stake out its difference from Dowland's in ways that are unapologetically iconoclastic.

Adès's decision to stand apart from Dowland's original so decisively is also reflected in how he chose to premiere the work. *Darknesse Visible* received its first performance in October 1992 at Franz Liszt's House in Budapest.[12] In this way, Adès obliquely invites us to consider how his approach might run in parallel to Liszt's work as a transcriber. In his book on Liszt's transcriptions, Jonathan Kregor has noted that articulating a separate identity from a source piece was one of the key goals of transcription for Liszt. Kregor forces this issue to a particular point when he writes that "Liszt understood transcription to be the creation of difference; that is, an act of violation of—even violence towards—the original."[13] *Darknesse Visible*—being an "explosion," after all—continues this theme of violence explicitly.

Adès's exploration of difference permeates other works in the glossary as well. For example, the conspicuously non-idiomatic writing Adès used to set the pop-ska band Madness's song "Cardiac Arrest" for chamber ensemble is central to the overall effect of the arrangement, and is perfectly in keeping with the paradigmatic dissonance that the London Meltdown Festival (for which it was written) seeks to cultivate.

Difference also creeps up as a priority in Adès's prose work, indicating how his glosses and essays can reveal a family of shared concerns. Adès's essay "'Nothing but Pranks and Puns': Janáček's Solo Piano Music," for example, focuses on the question of how irreducible foreignness can be represented musically. While not an arrangement itself, it rests comfortably among Adès's glosses insofar as it reflects Adès's interest in musical representations of foreignness and alterity. The essay was written while Adès was a Creative Arts Fellow at Trinity College Cambridge in the late 1990s, and does not only provide a view of what aspects of Janáček's music Adès finds particularly noteworthy. For a reader familiar with Adès's output, it also hints at moments in Adès's own compositions.[14] For example, Adès describes Janáček's approach to sonata form in his work *1.X.1905* as "idiosyncratic but exact," a phrase which could be applied equally well to Adès's own use of sonata form in the first movement of his Piano Quintet.[15]

The affinities between Adès's account of Janáček's piano music and his own approach to setting Dowland's song seem particularly salient. Adès's discussion of Janáček's use of harmonic deferrals, registral considerations, and musical riddles reveals a set of considerations that are similar to those from *Darknesse Visible*. Adès emphasizes the "orchestral" elements of Janáček's approach to the piano, and notes that Janáček's writing defied pitch-oriented analyses of his music. In his discussion of Janáček's *Na památku*, Adès writes:

> In *Na památku*, the importance of "orchestration" in establishing these objects cannot be exaggerated: the exact spacing of a chord, the weighting of its individual elements, the dynamic context, the precise register at which the pitch occurs; furthermore, "orchestration" more generally applied to the musical clothing of the enharmonic skeleton, for example long-term rhythmic rhymes.[16]

From a certain distance Adès's reading of Janáček is similar to his own musical reading of Dowland. The conspicuous octave displacement of *Darknesse Visible*, for example, suggested that he was interested in seeing the degree to which expanding the registral ambit of individual lines could provide a novel account of Dowland's piece. One might also note "orchestral" facets of Adès's approach to *Darknesse Visible* such as his choice to notate the work primarily on three staves, the use of multicolored notation to indicate the different voices, and the pervasive pianissimo tremolos which shimmer around the quoted material like a halo.

Adès also calls attention to Janáček's cunning use of enharmonic modulations: "Janáček's single most far-reaching quality . . . is still generally underestimated: the redefinition of structural tonality through an unprecedented concentration on ambiguous, and particularly enharmonic, key relationships."[17] The connection here between Janáček's smooth yet distorted voice leading and *Darknesse Visible* is not so direct, since Adès does not rely on enharmonic modulation in his work. But the affective consequences of some of Adès's choices in *Darknesse Visible*—for example his avoidance of predictable cadential movement—seem analogous to the overall effect he detects in Janáček's enharmonic twists and turns. Adès concludes his essay by ruminating about the potential of these enharmonic modulations to create uncanny sensations of paradox and alterity. Focusing on an irreconcilable harmonic clash in Janáček's *Vzpomínka* (Souvenir; 1928), Adès writes enigmatically that "otherness is persistent, a fact, as is failure; but a C-sharp can become a D-flat, and that is what is meant by humanity."[18] In this conclusion, Adès seems to suggest that relatively minor compositional decisions can carry enormous symbolic weight. Similarly, a more subtle aesthetic of difference also helps to illuminate Adès's decisions for other works in his glossary. Questions of idiom, phrasing, articulation, and instrumentation are full of affective import for Adès, and it is the devilish attention to these details which is the key to considering Adès's four arrangements of harpsichord pieces by Couperin.

Arrangements and Performance

In 2007, when asked what he liked about Couperin, Adès snorted, "His wig."[19] Such a comment betrays the impatience Adès felt with interviewers for roughly twenty years, what he has called "the torture of public interlocution."[20] But it also masks Adès's genuine and longstanding enthusiasm for Couperin. In 1995, Adès was quite emphatic when he described his "ideal day": "staying at home and playing the harpsichord works of Couperin—a new inspiration on every page."[21] Two of his arrangements are from Couperin's *Pieces de Clavecin*. *Les Baricades Mistérieuses* (1994) is for chamber ensemble, and *Three Studies from Couperin* (2006) is for small orchestra. As a performer, conductor, and impresario, Adès has also championed Couperin's music, programming it several times while he was artistic director at the Aldeburgh music festival, further underscoring his fondness for the composer.

Adès's arrangements of Couperin are instantly recognizable for those familiar with the originals; one reviewer missed the point when writing that Adès's works "add hardly anything to the keyboard miniatures."[22] It seems more productive to consider these arrangements as demonstrations of Adès's perspective on performing these pieces. In an archival recording of a recital Adès played in Vancouver in 2010 provided by the CBC, he subtly emphasizes how *Les Baricades Mistérieuses* becomes a fiendishly difficult study in precisely controlled attacks and releases once one is playing on a modern piano. The more gradual decay of a struck piano string, combined with a modern grand's capability for double escapement, allows for a skilled player to restrike a string without allowing the damper to fall. Adès's performance is virtuosically legato, stringing Couperin's rich texture together seamlessly with minimal use of the pedal. The amount of space in the line is the precise issue which is the most notationally apparent in Adès's setting of *Les Baricades Mistérieuses*. By explicitly adding eighth-note rests in the cello part, and alternating the accompaniment figure between the bass clarinet and the cello and bass, Adès creates a thinner texture than is necessarily implied by a literal reading of Couperin's notation (Example 1.6). As the piece goes on, the various melodic lines are tossed about the small ensemble, the varied timbres lending a greater sense of sonorous space. Although Adès described *Darknesse Visible* as "aerating" Dowland's song "In Darknesse Let Mee Dwell," the same description might also obtain for his transcription of *Les Baricades Mistérieuses*.[23]

Similarly, Adès's *Three Studies from Couperin* explores the potential for a larger performing ensemble to highlight aspects of phrasing and ornamentation from Couperin's original. This work relies on a larger ensemble: two flutes, clarinet in B-flat, bassoon, two horns, trumpet, percussion, and a pair of string orchestras. *Three Studies* and *Les Baricades* have come to form a suite of sorts in their public appearances following their completion: between 2006 and the end of 2012, *Les Baricades* has been programmed alongside *Three Studies* in eight of sixteen performances (*Three Studies* has its own independent life, with forty-five total performances reported by Adès's publisher Faber between 2006 and 2012). Like *Les Baricades Mistérieuses*, the movements of *Three Studies* are taken from Couperin's harpsichord suites: "Les Amusemens" (Second book, 7th Order); "Les Tours de Passe-passe" (Fourth book, 22nd Order); "L'Âme-en-Peine" (Third Book, 13th Order).

One striking aspect of Couperin's "Les Amusemens" is its intense degree of ornamentation, giving an otherwise stepwise diatonic melody a much more variegated contour. Adès emphasizes the centrality of this aspect of the piece through his orchestration. In Adès's setting, the movement opens with the alto flute and B-flat clarinet trading off the melody line, while the string orchestras each follow one or the other woodwind (Example 1.7). The second violins in each orchestra only play the ornaments, subtly supporting the two wind instruments. On a recording these nuances can be difficult to detect, not least because the alto flute and clarinet are playing in the same low register. In a live performance with the orchestras seated antiphonally, the visual effect of a call and response is made much more explicit than would be obvious from playing Couperin's original.[24] Later in the piece his deployment of the ornamentation becomes even more finely wrought, for example in the measure before rehearsal E, where, as the clarinet plays a concluding trill, the first violins in the respective orchestras split the ornament among themselves. Near the end of the work, Adès seems to comment on—or rather, redress—the peculiarities of the harpsichord, as well: while Couperin's original ending moves into the lowest ranges of the harpsichord, which almost always overpowers the treble on that instrument, Adès pares the texture near the end so that the movement eventually rolls to a stop as each instrument gradually drops out.

Example 1.6

a) Couperin, *Les Baricades Mistériueses*, mm. 1–9.

b) Adès, arr., Couperin, *Les Baricades Mistérieuses*, mm. 1–9. © 1994 Faber Music Ltd, reproduced by kind permission of the publishers.

Score in C (Adès's published score is transposed)

Example 1.7 Adès, arr., Couperin, *Les Amusemens*, mm. 1–5. From "Three Studies From Couperin," by Thomas Adès © 2006 Faber Music Ltd, reproduced by kind permission of the publishers.

Couperin's "Les Tours De Passe-passe" is a simple two-reprise form and in the style of a lively gigue. In Adès's setting, he splits the melody across the woodwinds (Example 1.8), but what is perhaps most striking is that he uses Couperin's initial ascending gesture as the basis for an ongoing accompaniment figure. By consistently accenting the second beat of each triplet subdivision in the pizzicato violas, Adès creates an energetic forward momentum in the rhythmic profile of the work, which is then "corrected" by having all of the instruments rhythmically square with one another at the cadence (Example 1.9). The offset beat at the

Example 1.8 Adès, arr., Couperin, *Les Tours de Passe-Passe*, mm. 1–11.

Example 1.9 Adès, arr., Couperin, *Les Tours de Passe-Passe*, mm. 38–41.

beginning is simply Adès's rearrangement of Couperin's musical material—giving away the surprise at the end of the first reprise at the beginning, so that one of the most novel aspects of Couperin's original is articulated at the beginning of Adès's arrangement.

Taken as a whole, Adès's arrangements of Couperin are subtle commentaries on the originals, and in this respect perform work similar to what arrangements have done for our view of other composers. For example, scholars have noted how Ravel's arrangements and transcriptions illuminated important facets of that composer's approach to the orchestra.[25] In Adès's case, his settings of Couperin's music are precise representations of the originals on one level but commentaries on another: articulation, orchestration, and in particular the choice to divide the strings into two separate orchestras gave Adès the ability to create many new possible configurations in the *Three Studies*. What really seems to emerge from Adès's arrangements of Couperin is not so much an extravagant reimagining of Couperin's original text, as was the case in *Darknesse Visible*. Rather, it is the manner in which the process of arrangement served as a means for Adès to explore possibilities that alternate performing ensembles create for emphasizing different aspects of a given work. In this light we might reconsider Adès's facetious comment about Couperin's wig, since in these arrangements it seems that Adès is taken with the kinds of interpretive decisions that would be central to a performer realizing the work. His arrangements of Couperin center on questions of performance, fashion, and style; perhaps Adès's scoff about Couperin's coiffure is not so wide of the mark.

Intensification

In *Full of Noises*, Adès noted, "I've never revised to 'tone things down.' Only the opposite: when the effect wasn't strong enough, only ever to make the effect stronger."[26] This trend is also apparent in his glossary in two pieces Adès wrote based on his own operas: *Court Studies* (2005) and *Concert Paraphrase on "Powder Her Face"* (2010). We will return to *Court Studies* when we consider *The Tempest*; for now the *Concert Paraphrase* provides more than enough demonstration of how Adès intensifies as he arranges.

Adès premiered the *Concert Paraphrase* himself at a series of concerts in March 2010. Not counting the *Mazurkas* (2009), it was the first time he had written for solo piano in more than a decade.[27] Adès explained the piece as follows:

For the *Concert Paraphrase* I have taken four scenes from my first opera, *Powder Her Face*, and freely transcribed them as a piano piece. The opera's libretto, by the novelist Philip Hensher, paints the portrait of a Duchess of a certain age at the end of the twentieth century and the end of British aristocratic influence. In the opera the Duchess's grace and glamour are figured in the music by a certain virtuosity which encouraged me to feel that parts of the music would translate into a piano Paraphrase rather in the manner of Liszt or Busoni.[28]

Adès then goes on to explain how the piece is assembled from four scenes of *Powder Her Face* (Table 1.3). He calls the first scene his "'Ode to Joy,'" since the Duchess is singing about her favorite perfume, *Joy*. This clunky pun on Adès's part is but the first in a huge array of allusive elements in the *Concert Paraphrase*. These allusions spilled out into the context of its premiere, harkening back to *Darknesse Visible*: Adès first played the *Concert Paraphrase* at the same Vancouver recital mentioned above, where he performed not only Couperin's *Les Baricades Misterieuses* but also recapitulated his other allegiances by including Janáček's *On an Overgrown Path*, Book 2 and Liszt's transcription of Wagner's *Liebestod* from *Tristan und Isolde*.

The second section of the *Concert Paraphrase* is based on Act 1, Scene 5 in the opera, in which the Duke is in the bedroom with his mistress, and reveals Adès's apparent delight in building tightly nested allusions that turn and fold in on one another, playing with listeners' expectations. One of the main themes from Scene 5 is a soaring melodic line accompanied by broken arpeggiations (Example 1.10). This tune is already ironic in its original presentation in *Powder Her Face*, drawing on a broadly spun out vocal style as the Duke sings "You know, they said we'd never see that style again, after the war. And here we are." It is one of several moments in the opera where Adès blurs the line between the diegetic and the non-diegetic, between the imaginary

Table 1.3 Adès, *Concert Paraphrase* Concordance with *Powder Her Face*

Concert Paraphrase	Scene	Notes
I	1	The Duchess's "Ode to Joy"
II	5	Truncated "Is Daddy Squiffy" sequence
III	3	Thoroughgoing transcription of "Fancy Being Rich" until p. 21, at which point an extended quasi cadenza
IV	8	"Ghost Epilogue" Rehearsal Z

Example 1.10 Adès, *Powder Her Face*, Scene 5, excerpt. By Thomas Adès and Philip Hensher © 2006 Faber Music Ltd, reproduced by kind permission of the publishers.

world of the opera's musical universe and tunes which the characters them-selves hear as part of their world.[29]

In the *Concert Paraphrase*, Adès showcases this moment in much the way that Liszt featured the most conspicuous tunes in some of his transcriptions (Example 1.11). By choosing this particular melody Adès nests the Duke's nostalgia within a thunderous reimagination of it for piano, which in turn evokes the entire tradition of virtuoso transcriptions of opera. Yet Adès's range of allusion and reference for this passage pushes outwards beyond the reuse of melodic material or a more generally evocative style. He also employs some

Example 1.11 Adès, *Concert Paraphrase on Powder Her Face*, II, excerpt. ©
2010 Faber Music Ltd, reproduced by kind permission of the publishers.

of the more recognizable signifiers of common-practice tonality to guide
this section to its abrupt end. Adès closes the second section of the *Concert
Paraphrase* with another rhapsodic passage which suggests a pedal on B, with
an underlying tonality of E, another quote of the Duke's tune, and then a passage which briefly suggests a retransition over a D dominant pedal (Example
1.12). This passage teases the listener, since there is nothing structurally significant about G or E major for this section of the *Concert Paraphrase*. More
to the point, this passage does not retransition to anything: the movement
abruptly ends rather than restating existing material. In other words, Adès
uses two kinds of dominant prolongation to signal the impending arrival of a

Example 1.12 Adès, *Concert Paraphrase on Powder Her Face*, II, ending.

long-range harmonic event, but ultimately frustrates both. In so doing, Adès uses a different set of techniques in the *Concert Paraphrase* to heighten the disorientation that the kaleidoscopic use of styles engenders in listeners to the original passage from *Powder Her Face*.

In this passage of the *Concert Paraphrase*, Adès isolates, intensifies, and reimagines particular compositional strategies present in the original works. In the former, the distinct sound worlds of each character form the structural basis for the entire arrangement for chamber ensemble. In the latter, Adès's apparent glee at manipulating both introversive and extroversive musical signifiers has become one of the most potent expressive devices of this section of the *Concert Paraphrase*.[30] Of course, isolation and intensification also require careful selection of what to omit, and still other moments in his arrangements—including *Concert Paraphrase*—indicate the degree to which Adès understands how to create meaning through omissions of various types.

Absences

There are moments in Adès's glossary where he seems to note the mechanistic quality of translation—that long held, if problematic, desire for translators to move without friction from one medium to another. The analogy is imperfect, as analogies tend to be: a linguistic translation renders an utterance intelligible to an audience that might not have understood the text in its original form; Adès's musical "translations" remain intended for the same concert-going audience as their sources. At issue in both contexts, however, is that there is always a perspective from which the copy is not a *mere* copy; some additional signifying material is always introduced. In Adès's case, some of his most seemingly straightforward and innocuous copies are the very moments where he confronts the eerily mechanical quality of translation most explicitly.

Adès threw down the mechanistic gauntlet particularly forcefully when he decided to arrange two of Conlon Nancarrow's studies for player piano for two pianos. The music theorist Eric Drott has explored how Nancarrow's most extreme studies embrace a kind of mechanical sublime, a use of the technology of the player piano to create rhythmic relationships so intricate that the listener's capacity to process the counterpoint is overwhelmed and transported to a simple state of awe by the music's complexity.[31] The whole project of Nancarrow's player piano studies was to render playable what was ostensibly unplayable—for example rhythmic canons at the ratio of 2: √2. A central question of Adès's transcription, then, is how he moves in the opposite direction and makes what is unplayable playable.

In his review of Kyle Gann's book about Nancarrow's music, Adès gives some consideration to this question of performativity. "The early Studies," Adès writes,

> up to and including the comprehensive, symphonic No. 7, are hostages to the same immediacy of appeal; for sheer charm, no other post-war works of any technical ambition can approach them. To overexploit this quality, as do Yvar Mikhashoff's primped (and mistake-strewn) instrumentations, is to pasteurize the originals . . . and to mislead the listener into treating them as though digestible in large numbers, like Romantic miniatures; whereas each has an implosive density of substance, and requires concentration as particular as any individual classical symphony.[32]

This idea of "particular concentration" for these studies is especially evident in Adès's transcription of the sixth study. In Nancarrow's original, a not-quite-isorhythm undergirds the structure. In this case it is a fifteen-note *color* with a sixteen note *talea*, which is notated by Nancarrow across two staves. He cheats once in a while on the *talea*, and the two staves are in a 4:5 rhythmic relationship, with four notes alternating on each staff, lending the entire bass an intelligibility, but also a wobbliness. Above this not-quite ostinato, Nancarrow uses what Kyle Gann has called a "cowboy" tune in the treble, which is put through a few different variations over the course of the short piece.[33]

Adès begins his version with what would seem to be the most performer-friendly approach. Piano I takes the treble melody, and Piano II takes the complex accompaniment which on its own is tricky—the player must alternate between highly syncopated divisions of the bar in four and five—but not impossible. The baffling moment comes in m. 152 of Adès's setting, when the

Example 1.13 Adès, arr., Nancarrow Study #6 for Player Piano, mm. 152–69.

second piano begins playing the melody, which the first piano could accommodate (Example 1.13). The second piano, with little fanfare, has suddenly been plunged into a polyrhythmic thicket, as the player must now negotiate dividing the bar in 3, 4, 5, and 10 simultaneously.

For the second pianist, if not a listener in the hall, the piece has become significantly more difficult without any overtly noticeable change in the texture.

One is left wondering why Adès notated this passage as he did: if not to furnish a sort of hidden virtuosity for the second pianist, then perhaps as a private joke where one player must negotiate a tricky vertigo which belies the continuity of the musical surface. If, in Drott's mind, the mechanical sublime in Nancarrow's music was in the ear of the beholder, here Adès asks one performer in the ensemble to play at the limit of what some pianists might find to be an insurmountable technical challenge. In the commercially available recording of this piece, Adès plays second piano, leaving him alone as the private participant in this joke.[34]

The central paradox in arranging Nancarrow's player piano studies for real pianists is that it brings humans into an expressive world that was predicated on their absence; Ades's insertion of himself alone on the recording at this point only serves to underscore the effort to reduce or eliminate humans from these moments. It is not the only time that Adès has toyed with adding and removing human agency where we might not expect it. In the third section of the *Concert Paraphrase* he celebrates a different kind of mechanism, where that which appears to be human is unmasked and shown to be something else altogether.

The third section of Adès's *Concert Paraphrase* brings together all of the different threads of Adès's glossary—difference, intensification, polymathy, and absence—in a single passage. It is based on the third scene of the opera, in which a waitress sings the aria "Fancy Being Rich" while picking up after the Duke and Duchess's wedding. Even in the original opera, the scene portrays a character who is eerily inhuman. In *Powder Her Face*, "Fancy Being Rich" is sung by a waitress who is fantasizing about things that she seems not to want, animated by a joyless litany of what being wealthy could provide (Example 1.14). At the end of the scene, Hensher's libretto makes explicit what Adès's relentlessly repeated figures and the waitress's joyless, empty laughing have been telling us throughout the scene when the waitress sings "I wouldn't want to be happy if I was as rich as her."

The corresponding section in the *Concert Paraphrase* achieves its uncanny effect precisely through elimination of the vocal part (Example 1.15). This passage calls to mind Carolyn Abbate's theory about how the absence of the voice in an instrumental work can invite the perception that the performer—especially a virtuoso performer—is merely a marionette for the composer's wishes.[35] By the seemingly simple decision not to include the waitress's vocal part, Adès amplifies this quality of a conspicuous absence of humans, calling attention to the uneasy rapport of mechanism and virtuosity that troubles Abbate and others.[36]

Example 1.14 Adès, *Powder Her Face*, Scene 3, excerpt.

The interpretation of the waitress's absence from this passage of the paraphrase as an intensification of the inhuman is further supported by the presence of Liszt's transcription of the *Liebestod* on the program in which this
work was premiered. In that transcription, Isolde's vocal part is all but absent.
Jonathan Kregor interpreted Liszt's decision to include only a brief quote of
Isolde's melody as an enjoinder to "the audience to consider something beyond its realm of senses," a deepening of the mystical transfiguration which
Isolde undergoes at the end of the opera.[37] But in *Full of Noises*, Adès sees
Tristan und Isolde completely differently: "Wagner's music is fungal . . . it's a
sort of unnatural growth . . . [Tristan and Isolde are] taking drugs, aren't they?

Example 1.15 Adès, *Concert Paraphrase on Powder Her Face*, III, excerpt.

It's artificial. They're not really that keen on each other. I can hear it in the music, it's inorganic."[38] Put another way, Adès reads the ending of *Tristan und Isolde* not as a moment of transcendence, but as an apotheosis of artifice. By nevertheless recruiting Liszt's strategy of vocal redaction into his own *Concert Paraphrase*, Adès advances an altogether novel method for portraying the waitress's patent automatism. In this moment Adès rhymes in two different languages, two parallel currents of meaning, at the same time.

This passage also allows us to at least consider the possibility of a rapport between Adès's glossary and Adès's father, to counterbalance the discussions of his mother—Dawn Ades, an expert on surrealist art—which have permeated his public reception.[39] Timothy Ades is a poet and translator, and an author of lipograms, a kind of restricted form of writing where a letter or group of letters is avoided. [40] In one example on his website, Timothy has reworded Shakespeare's sonnet 18 without using the letter *e*, so that the line "And every fair from fair sometime declines" becomes "And all fair fowls fall foul of you–know–what."[41] The points of contact between the *Paraphrase* and the lipogram are perhaps instructive: both can be considered translations, paradoxically, into the original language (for Timothy, one English poem to another; for Thomas one musical work to another); both seem to expect a reader or listener who can hold both the original and reimagined texts in their head simultaneously for maximum meaning; and while Timothy's is perhaps a bit more playful than Thomas's is at first blush, both doggedly pursue their goal to the end. While I would stop short of suggesting that Adès's music acts out some kind of Freudian family romance between his mother's surrealism and his father's virtuosically carefree translations, I do think that the glossary of Adès *fils* allows us to at least consider his father's role in his intellectual and aesthetic development, a dimension which in itself is an absence in the critical discourse surrounding Adès's music.

* * *

Readers who take a long historical view might yawn at Adès's glossary and say that nothing is new under the sun. Does Adès's glossary, in the end, really differ that much from nineteenth-century practices of musical reproduction, which perhaps reached their height in Liszt's body of transcriptions? Kregor's conceptual framework for Liszt's transcriptions is wide-ranging in its view, exploring not only the "violence" in Liszt's transcriptions, but also their qualities of physicality (in Berlioz), myth-making (in Beethoven), rivalry (with Wagner), as well as their affinities with Humboldt's theories of translation, to name just a few themes.[42] Adès's works considered here form a winding but ultimately parallel path to many of the issues that Kregor raises with regard to Liszt.

Adès's glossary cannot be characterized as merely reheated Liszt, if only because of the obvious fact that we do not live in the nineteenth century. Even if we accept the paradigm of the concert hall as a musical museum which allows for the anachronistic juxtaposition of practices across the centuries (something Adès himself does frequently in his life as a concert programmer), it would be a mistake not to insist on the historical particularity of the present moment and Adès's position therein. In her recent review of Kregor's book, Francesca Brittan astutely notes that Liszt's transcriptions have labored under a modernist bias against reproduction most forcefully articulated by Walter Benjamin.[43] While Brittan points out that Benjamin's emphasis on originality has been retroactively applied to the era before mechanical reproduction, Adès's return to these practices reflects the slow erosion of modernism's harsher imperatives about progress, autonomy, and originality over the past few decades in the composition world. One could point to Michael

Finnissy's arrangements of Gershwin and others, or the pianist Anthony de Mare's *Liaisons* project, in which thirty-six composers have provided "re-imaginations" of the songs of Stephen Sondheim, as just two examples of this more recent, broader embrace of arrangement and associated practices.

Even though Adès's work with existing music participates in larger contemporary trends, Adès's glossary should enjoy a special status for a few reasons. Although *Full of Noises* advances responses to many questions about Adès's aesthetics, the elaborate web of metaphors he employs in discussions of his own music often leaves one puzzled. In the space of two pages, for example, he compares material from his Piano Quintet to a hallway, a city, "grit in an oyster," and "a child learning about its environment."[44] In this passage, as with others in the book, Adès guides the reader through a hall of mirrors of different metaphors bouncing off one another, with little specific anchoring to the musical texts. This is indicative of a larger trend on Adès's part to not discuss his own music too much, hence differentiating him from many composers who eagerly discuss their works at length. I think that the argument could be made that Adès's extensive use of existing music can help us to understand some of his priorities as a composer, in the absence—or ambiguity—of his own commentary.

The works in Adès's glossary are understandably considered minor in his output compared to his larger orchestral pieces and operas. These works nevertheless illuminate elements of Adès's sensibility in a way that his more celebrated pieces do not and moreover that they offer another way of understanding the boundary-crossing for which he is so well known. They also provide a unique vantage point for contemplating Adès's relatively special position in the contemporary composition scene, given his first-rate qualifications as a performer alongside his significant career as a composer. Although there are other composer/performer and composer/conductor hybrids active today, few would argue that there are vast ranks of composers today who could likely enjoy top-flight careers as pianists and conductors independent of their own music. In this sense the works considered here, and their liminal status between composition, performance, and analysis, constitute a particularly singular vein of material in the case of Adès. If Adès's glossary can carry all this weight—to illuminate his priorities, define aspects of his aesthetics which are otherwise obscure, and provide an integrated view of his work as a composer, conductor, and pianist—then these works (and similar ones that may join the glossary as Adès continues to write) deserve consideration in any account of his contributions to the musical life of the twenty-first century.

2
The Twelve Tones

> Pattern is a very powerful thing, yet it mustn't be so powerful that it's
> the only thing in the music.
>
> —Thomas Adès

Introduction

Throughout his career, Thomas Adès's music has been seen by commentators as employing sophisticated technical tools while remaining accessible enough to attract a broad audience. Even as early as 1994, the music critic Norman Lebrecht wrote, "While Avant-gardism used to mean squeaky wheels and serialist formulae, Adès and his generation make music that is meant to be enjoyed."[1] Although Adès has expressed concern about some of his compositions going down *too* easily, his music remains a body of work which has enjoyed popular success in part because many listeners take something from the very first hearing.[2]

At the same time, Lebrecht's mention of serialism is particularly telling. Adès has drawn on serialist procedures throughout his career, although with increasing frequency since 2000. While John Roeder has noted the presence of a tone row in the final movement of *Arcadiana* (1995), the bulk of the serialist works date from after *The Tempest* and include *In Seven Days* (2008), *Lieux Retrouvés* (2009), *Mazurkas* (2009), *Polaris* (2010), and *The Four Quarters* (2010).[3] This chapter explores Adès's engagement with serialism and its history as one of the twentieth century's most touted compositional techniques. Its presence in these works is not only a consistent theme but also one part of a larger hybrid compositional strategy. Adès seldom presents a row as the unequivocal building block of a piece or movement. Instead, it is used in combination with other techniques ranging from isorhythm (*The Four Quarters*), to developing variation (*In Seven Days*), to a more wide-ranging set of techniques which Adès has described as "magnetic" (*Polaris*). Such a use not only aligns Adès with other strands of compositional practice found in twentieth-century British music (to which we shall return), but also allows these works to avoid

Thomas Adès in Five Essays. Drew Massey, Oxford University Press (2021). © Oxford University Press.
DOI: 10.1093/oso/9780199374960.001.0001.

Lebrecht's dreaded "serialist formulae" yet nevertheless leave us with the fact of their basis in a family of compositional practices that have symbolically loomed large in the historiography of twentieth-century music.

Lebrecht's polemical comment—especially its far-from-inevitable contrast between serialism and "music that is meant to be enjoyed"—also points to a conceptual slippage that is common in writing on serialism, namely that serialism presupposes ugliness. In its most common usage, the term serialism—meaning a composer's choice to organize a musical texture around an ordering of pitches that (typically) uses all twelve notes of the chromatic scale—describes a structural rather than a semiotic or hermeneutic characteristic of a given composition.[4] Lebrecht's shorthand notwithstanding, discussing a work in terms of its serialist features can tell us how a piece is assembled, but cannot wholly determine how a piece is encountered as an aesthetic object.[5] Arved Ashby has offered one path out of this apparent gap between signifier and signified by proposing that we consider twelve-tone methodologies as heuristics which guide but do not determine overall meaning either for the composer or listener.[6] In Ashby's argument, twelve-tone composition is best considered an "ideal type"—a concept, like the "classical style" in Charles Rosen's formulation, that guides our understanding of a repertoire but is seldom perfectly exemplified in a particular musical work. Ashby's view allows an encounter with a work which embraces multiple layers of meaning at once: the note-to-note technical procedures, the ideological and political ramifications of adopting serialism, as well as the intertextual resonances that ring out when a contemporary composer relies on a technique as fraught as serialism. These multiple layers of possible meaning are part of the challenge in considering the role of serialism in Adès's music.

It is one of the contradictions of Adès's work that he relies on extensive formalist procedures—not just serialism, but also fugue (*In Seven Days*), passacaglia (*Concentric Paths; The Tempest*), and rhythmic canon (*Lieux Retrouvés; Asyla; Concentric Paths*)—but has also taken care to distance himself from the arch-modernism of the previous century. Commenting on *In Seven Days*, Adès suggested that refusing sensuous pleasure was a bit quaint: "Why would anyone be ashamed of beauty? It's a very 20th-century idea that you might be. Thankfully that's gone."[7] Nevertheless, Adès's occasional engagement with serialism is where we find some of his most direct compositional confrontations with the longstanding tensions between expression and technique, surface and structure, subject and object. Serialism may *denote* a technique, but in Adès's music it *connotes* a constellation of cultural meanings. This distinction is often lost because of the heavy, even deterministic, symbolic baggage that serialism has accumulated in the last century, as well as the success that some practitioners of serialism have had in describing the technique as the necessary—even inevitable—consequence of historical forces.[8] It isn't surprising, therefore, to find that serial techniques fulfill many different affective purposes in Adès's music, purposes which may be more or less situated on a spectrum based on the intelligibility of the formal procedures to a listener. It seems unlikely that Adès will provide—or even would like for listeners to have—a fixed meaning for these or any of his works. When asked about his relationship to listeners in the recently published book of interviews with the British journalist Tom Service, titled *Full of Noises*, Adès responded: "I'm not thinking about the private responses of individual audience members. That would be presumptuous."[9] Adès's stance gives a listener (or, at least, a listener who would defer to authorial intention in the first place) the leave to encounter these pieces as he or she likes, with or without serialism's historicist gravity. Taken as a whole, these works are emblematic of Adès's complex relationship with modernism, his ongoing conversation with the recent musical past, and his frequent use of seemingly effortlessly lush musical surfaces which float above extremely complex technical means.[10]

Serialism's Shadow

It would be difficult to overstate the symbolic role serialism has played in histories of twentieth-century music.[11] While some authors have explored alternative pathways through modernism, many have bemoaned serialism's perceived hegemony as a technique and means of continuing concert music's march toward ultimate abstraction (and hence "liberation").[12] In the hands of its more analytical practitioners after the Second World War such as Boulez, Babbitt, and Stockhausen, serialism rests comfortably as the destination point in historiographies of Western music that have emphasized technical innovation as the ultimate criterion for the historical significance of a given composer's output.

Serialism's birth also saw a reconfiguration of a composer's relationship with the audience, and Adès's serialist works—like virtually all other serial works—raise the question of salience: that is, whether serial techniques are really audible, and regardless of whether they are or not, if it should matter to audiences. Theodor Adorno speculated on the possibility of an "expert" listener, one who would be able to incorporate even the most obscure technical procedures into their listening experience. In *Introduction to the Sociology of Music*, Adorno envisioned a listener "who innately misses nothing, and is able to account for what is being heard immediately, at any moment."[13] For his part, Arnold Schoenberg was at times suspicious about whether an audience needed to peek behind the curtain at all. One example of this aspect of Schoenberg's stance was his well-known 1932 letter to Rudolf Kolisch, scolding the violinist for attempting to determine the row in the Third String Quartet, writing that such efforts "only lead to what I have always been dead against: seeing how it is *done*; whereas I have always helped people to see how it *is*."[14] Such debates about what listeners can or should do when confronted with modernist music were also considered at Schoenberg's Society for Private Musical Performances. While the Society predated serialism by several years, its hostility toward music as a spectacle for enjoyment or criticism helped to lay the groundwork for the more polemically scientific attitudes of later serialists. More recently, serialist methods have been in the crosshairs of a more general critique of any compositional technique—or analytical worldview—that might presume to offer universal and binding accounts of musical meaning.[15] In other words, serialism and responses to serialism both raise a host of questions about how an audience might relate to a work, and an audience's obligation to attend to (or defiantly ignore) a piece's method of construction.

Some recent scholarship has shed light on the shaky origins of what has come to be such an iconic technique, and Adès's own equivocal embrace of serialism recapitulates aspects of Alban Berg's and Anton Webern's early serialist efforts. Arved Ashby and Anne Shreffler authored landmark essays on Berg and Webern, respectively, in the mid-1990s. Through an examination of the sketches of Berg's *Lyric Suite*, Ashby showed how that work constituted an ambivalent engagement with Schoenberg's notions about writing with all twelve tones, and how it struck a delicate balance between free atonality and twelve-tone writing.[16] Similarly, Shreffler considered Webern's songs written between 1922 and 1925, demonstrating his problematic absorption of Schoenberg's technique, and writing that "a central paradox of Webern as a twelve-tone composer is that the Schoenberg disciple long considered to be the most 'advanced' practitioner of the method was the one who initially resisted it the most."[17] Both Shreffler's and Ashby's arguments proceed through assiduous reconstruction of Webern's and Berg's respective compositional approaches by painstakingly combing through the composers' sketch materials and other archival materials.

Since Adès's hybrid approach to serialism seemed reminiscent of Berg's and Webern's, I initially expected that my consideration of Adès's twelve-tone works would yield to an approach similar to that of Ashby and Shreffler. The particulars of Adès's working methods, as well as his position as a twenty-first-century composer, however, have suggested that a different approach to his music is in order. First of all, there is no archive of Adès's papers beyond what he himself has retained.[18] Similarly, Adès sometimes develops material by recording short ideas from an electronic keyboard as a "very crude tool for layering." These short recordings are also destroyed as part of the process: "I delete most of them as I go along, and all of them when I finish a piece . . . What ends up on the page has barely any relation to these recordings."[19] Second, the chronological gap that separates Adès from Berg and Webern is filled with the consequences of the second Viennese school, what Alexander Goehr (one of Adès's teachers) has called the "Paris-Darmstadt-Princeton mode" of "hard-line serialism."[20] As a result, Adès—like all twenty-first-century composers—writes from the perspective of having seen many of the consequences of the innovations of the Second Viennese School. Taken together, the source situation for Adès in particular, and the inherent self-consciousness required for a twenty-first-century composer to write serially in general, create a peculiar critical nexus. Although Adès may, at some point in the future, discuss in more detail the technical language of these works, what they meant to him at the time of composition may already be lost. Nevertheless, between his interviews, the reception of these works, and the published scores themselves, there is enough to hazard a reading which considers how these works trade in the affective consequences of his approach to serialism.

Adès seems to have little patience for most serialist music written after the Second Viennese School. When Tom Service remarked to Adès that "the will to create pattern at all costs . . . now seems a strange obsession for music to have had," Adès replied: "I've actually become much more serial—certainly not in the kind of Schoenbergian sense, but when you're dealing with twelve notes and how they balance magnetically, serial thinking is at the end of that somewhere."[21] This passage is the only mention of Schoenberg in Adès and Service's entire book, and Webern only rates a mention for his use of cowbells in *Five Pieces for Orchestra*. Moreover, Adès's discussion of Stockhausen and Boulez in *Full of Noises* indicates why he has so little interest in the postwar avant-garde:

The more I looked into the music of Stockhausen the more I felt it just seemed like a flower that had died months before and was still on the shelf in a vase . . . [*Licht*] seemed to be driven more by some kind of dilemma that he'd got himself into, that he was born into, that he'd emerged into, whatever it was, some artistic conundrum . . . It seemed to me that the only thing that mattered was that he had theoretically to dominate; it didn't especially matter how. And that, to me, is uninteresting. The same feeling, slightly, stays with me about Boulez, although I was more struck by the actual music, but tended to feel generally the works were unnecessarily long. I still do, actually. I can't say they had, how shall I put it, irresistible allure.[22]

If Adès's critique of Boulez and Stockhausen is aimed at a more general experience of their music, perhaps the most famous example of serialism in British music prior to Adès— Britten's *Turn of the Screw*—is particularly problematic for Adès. He considered the work "dilettantish," and raged openly:

> I feel Britten puts that structural scheme in *The Turn of the Screw* so that critics or whoever could say "Ah, structure!" and feel that they are in on the joke. That's what a British critic, forgive me, would think. It makes them feel clever, people who swallow and regurgitate received ideas but don't look at what they mean ... In contrast to the formal things in Berg's *Lulu*, which are so transcended and overgrown that they cease to advertise themselves. But they give such depth to *Lulu* ... In *Turn of the Screw* the formal conceits only show up the one-dimensionality of the piece. It's embarrassing that the title tells you exactly what the music is going to do. That's hobbyish.[23]

Adès's contempt for Britten in this passage seems to obscure the more substantive affinities Adès's approach to serialism might have with other British composers. Nowhere does Adès discuss Peter Maxwell Davies or Alexander Goehr in *Full of Noises*, but some serial works by Davies, at least, seem to reflect the compositional priorities that Adès puts on display in his own.[24] For example, Davies's decision to use the first part of a row and its own inversion (P_0 and I_0) in concert with one another to create sense of tonal hierarchy in Five Pieces for Piano, Op. 2, no. 1, is exactly the approach we will see below in Adès's *Polaris*. Similarly, Davies's delight in charting new paths through a row matrix, as he does in *Ave Maris Stella*, is similar to the process Adès uses in *In Seven Days*.[25] Considering how comparatively insular Britain's talent system for composers was in the twentieth century, Adès's silence on his immediate forebears from the Manchester School is noteworthy and could be interpreted variously as diplomatic deference to them or as a sort of internalized anxiety about his compositional inheritance; his withering language about Britten's opera only serves to underscore this psychological dimension of his commentary.[26] At the same time, Adès's cosmopolitanism today suggests we ought not over-emphasize a British-only historical reference point; his work *Polaris* helps to underscore the various approaches that Adès has taken in terms of working with serial textures.

Polaris and "Magnetic" Serialism

The central metaphor Adès used to describe his large orchestral work *Polaris: Voyage for Orchestra* is "magnetism," and although it is not the first of his works which he has identified as serial, it is the most approachable. He has done little to explain how the ideas of magnetism and serialism might interact, except to note that *Polaris* "doesn't make the kind of noise that the word [i.e., "serialism"] implies."[27] He also hinted at a certain fluidity in his approach to serialism when he wrote that "I have a problem—well, it's not a problem for me, but it can make life confusing talking to anyone else—which is that I don't believe at all in the official distinction between tonal and atonal music. I think the only way to understand these things is that they are the result of magnetic forces within the notes, which create a magnetic tension, an attraction or repulsion ... In *Polaris*, I had to transfer meaning from the C-sharp to the A."[28] Since Adès does not provide any more technical explanation than this, we are left on our own to try to determine how these tensions actually work within the musical texture of the piece.

Exceedingly clear arrangement of material, together with additive structures, are the primary means by which Adès avoids making the "noise" that he associates with twelve-tone writing. *Polaris* is organized as an ABA' form, with the tonal centers of C-sharp, G, and then A (Example 2.1). The initial statements of the material set up the central premises of Adès's "magnetic" approach to serialism. The flutes state the basic material that the winds and strings draw on (Example 2.2) as an accompaniment figure, undergirding the primary melodic development that takes place first in the trumpets and then throughout the brass section (Example 2.3). In both examples, C-sharp is repeated frequently, allowing that pitch to assert itself as the tonal center in the texture; the centrality of C-sharp is only reinforced by the stepwise motion back to it in both the melody and the accompaniment. For their first five pitches, the melodies in Examples 2.2 and 2.3 are also inversions of one another. Since all inversions of pentatonic material are themselves pentatonic, when considered independently the melody and accompaniment have the free flowing, chime-like quality of a pentatonic scale.

Adès creates musical tension in *Polaris* by manipulating these additive structures. The flute passage in Example 2.2 features two additional pitches— D and C—attached to the end of the collection, and this two-note asymmetry between the melodic and harmonic collections disrupts the "expected" development of the work on several levels. First, only eleven of the twelve pitches are played—G-natural is missing. Secondly, the asymmetry means that the melodic and harmonic collections are tantalizingly close to one another, since if the C were moved from the end of the accompaniment and added to the brass material, the two resulting hexachords would be in perfect inversion. To return to Adès's imagery of the "magnetic," if the pentatonic collection is the field in which the music moves, then it is charged by this asymmetrical setup.

This asymmetry exists alongside the striking discipline of the writing along other lines. By almost any criteria one might choose—rhythm, register, pitch,

Example 2.1 Adès, *Polaris*, pitch material. © 2010 Faber Music Ltd, reproduced by kind permission of the publishers.

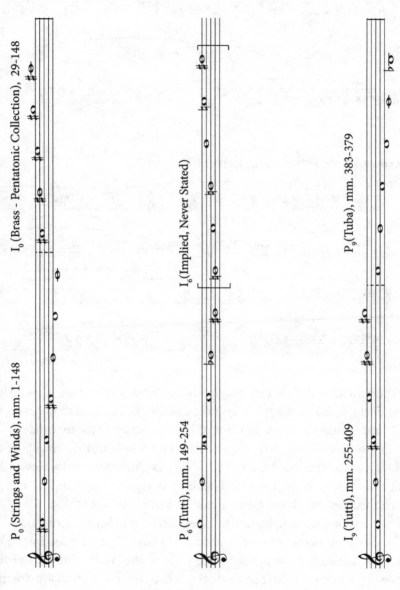

Example 2.2 Adès, *Polaris*, flute I & II, mm. 14–28.

Example 2.3 Adès, *Polaris*, trumpet, mm. 29–63.

or orchestration—Adès is remarkably strict about developing the brass melody from Example 2.3 in the first section of *Polaris*. As Table 2.1a indicates, once the trumpet enters at rehearsal C (m. 29), the structure of the remainder of the opening section (through m. 148) is driven by subsequent statements of this melody, each adding one brass voice and each beginning one octave lower than the previous statement. The tune is ultimately repeated four times (trumpet, then horns, then trombone, then horns again), each time with thicker doublings. These entries are also emphasized by Adès's decision to bar the score so that the melody's strong notes fall on downbeats. Moreover, once a brass instrument states the material, it orbits around the same pitches with minimal variation. While these statements have some rhythmic ebb and flow, they cleave closely to the prevailing pace set by the lead instrument for a statement of the tune. Finally, at rehearsal G, the tuba enters, playing the inversion of this tune at the very floor of the orchestra's register with the double basses and contraforte (Example 2.4).

Since this melody lacks a tritone, it makes the arrival of the G-natural— the only pitch missing for a statement of the total chromatic collection, and a diminished fifth away from the tonal center of C-sharp—all the more striking at the beginning of the second section in m. 149. This middle section follows a somewhat similar process of developing the material in the brass, although this time it uses the inversion of the original brass material (what might be called P_6 in a tone-row matrix, and is given in Example 2.5).

The final section, the third part in the musical triptych, returns to the arrangement of pitch material from the first section, this time with A as the pitch center (Table 2.1b). In the third section, however, the original brass melody is extended to include a final phrase which reaches all the way to G-sharp (Example 2.6). In this way, Adès's pitch material is now symmetrically deployed across two hexachords (Example 2.1, bottom row) that are inversions of one another, and the piece lumbers to a close on a strongly stated chord that includes all twelve pitches, with an A, approached from E-flat (again a tritone from the central pitch), marking both the highest and lowest note in the final chord.

In other words, there are some aspects of Adès's "magnetism" which are achieved by fairly conventional strategies, such as pitch repetition, and postponing completion of the aggregate. Adès's approach in this work is also noteworthy for the way in which it engages earlier conceptions of how twelve-tone material might be developed. Adorno spoke of the "didactic exemplary" character of Schoenberg's later work, as if Schoenberg were trying to demonstrate for other composers, as well as analysts, all the possible consequences of this twelve-tone technique.[29] In a distinct but comparable vein, the musical material in *Polaris* unfolds so systematically that it almost seems as if Adès is trying to teach the listener a tone row, one pitch at a time. At the same time, the repetitive qualities of *Polaris* also challenge ideas about the supposed "efficiency" that serialist works could achieve in communicating a composer's ideas.[30] We might also speak admiringly of other aspects of the work's "restraint" (as the composer Nico Muhly has of Adès's output as a whole) by noting Adès's thorough use of a single row, and the use of only two operations—transposition and inversion—on it.[31] At the same time, *Polaris* also relies on serialist techniques that emphasize priorities other than "efficiency" and "didacticism." Schoenberg would never have written the melodies Adès used in Examples 2.2 and 2.3 in a twelve-tone composition, if for no other reason than their insistent return to C-sharp. Put another way, Adès's choice of music material allows him to have the discipline of serialism alongside the accessibility of other modes of pitch organization: this hexachord is also particularly suited for writing in a style which implies tonality, since it is in effect a pentatonic scale.[32]

Finally, the fact that Adès announced *Polaris*'s serialism at all ought to be considered. Why did Adès go through the trouble of such finely wrought serial techniques in *Polaris* when the overall effect is similar to minimalist and post-minimalist works which do not necessarily place such strict constraints

Table 2.1a Adès, *Polaris*: Melodic Layout, mm. 29–148

Rehearsal	Melodic Range (Brass)	Doubling	C♯	D♯	C♯	E♯	D♯	C♯	G♯
C	Tpt. 1–3	C♯5–A♯5	18	23.5	5	26(2)	12(2)	6	24(1)
D	Horns 1,3	Cello	6	11	6	12(4.5)	11	6	5(6)
	Tpt. 1–3		0	0	4.5	6(6)	12	6	10.5(6)
E	Horns 1,3		0	0	6	6(4)	7(6)	6	4(4)
	Tpt. 1–3	Ob. 1,2	5(3)	4	0	4	6(6)	4(7) D♯4	8(4)
	Tbn 1,2	Vcl.	6	7(4)	6	6(4)	7(8)	4	7(3)
F	Horns 1,3	Bsn.	3(7)	4	0	3(3)	0	3(8) D♯3	3(4)
	Horns 2,4	Bs. Cl., Hp., Vcl., D.B.	5	4(9)	3	3(3)	4(3)	3	4(4)
	Tpt. 1–3	Ob.	0	0	5(4)	3	5(3)	6	8(8)
	Tbn 1,2	Vcl.	0	0	0	0	0	3	3(4)
G	Horns 1,3	Bsn.	0	0	6(7)	3	6(5)	9	10(3)
	Horns 2,4	Vcn. B.Cl.	0	0	3	6(4)	3(9)	9	5(4)
	Tpt. 1–3	Ob./Cl.	6(10)	6	7(4)	4(8)	7(3)	3	3(16)
	Tbn		3(15)	3	0	5(4)	0	5(18) D♯4	3(3)
	Tuba (Plays Inversion)	D.B. C. Forte	6 C♯	10(6) B	5 C♯	4(5) A	12(3) B	9 C♯	14(8) F♯

Numbers in Parenthesis signify rests. All durations are in eighth notes.

The passages are barred according to the instruments in **bold**.

Vertically running text indicates interpolated notes.

E♯	D♯	C♯	A♯	G♯	E♯	D♯	C♯	Statement Duration (with rests)	Total Statement Duration	m. 149
6	14 (3)	0	25.5	15 (2)	7	22.5	0 (3)	204.5 (13)	217.5	
5	8.5(15)	0	9	6 (2.5)	5	9	0	99.5 (28)	127.5	
5	4.5(2.5)	5	9 (3)	7.5	0	7 (5)	0			
3	8 (2)	14	7 (1)	4	0	7 (3)	7			
5	0	7(5) | D♯7	5(10)	12(10)	5	5(4)	0			
7	7 (10)	0	10	5 (5)	6	6 (14)	0	84 (48)	132	
4	0	4(3) | D♯6	6 (5)	4	4 (3)	4 | E♯6(7)	0			
4	3 (12)	0	5	4	3	4 (10)	0	49 (41)	90	
8 (4)	9	6	5 (4)	7 (3)	6	4 (3)	0			G♮
4	3 (3)	8	7	6(3) | C♯8	8(3)	4 (6)	0			
9 (7)	8	4	4 (10)	7 (19)	4	8 (12)	4			
4	4(9)	10	11	4 (2)	0	0	0			
4	4 (4)	6 (7)	14	9 (8)	9	3 (4)	0	85 (64)	149	
6	0	7(4) | D♯3	4(4) | C♯6(4)	4	0	14 | E♯5(29)	4			
6 A	7 (9) B	5 C♯	5 (4) E	5 F♯	6 (3) A	6 (4) B	0	100 (42)	142	

Example 2.4 Adès, *Polaris*, tuba, mm. 130–48.

Example 2.5 Adès, *Polaris*, trumpet, mm. 164–82.

on the transformation of pitch material? A few answers are possible. The single-mindedness of the working out of the material in *Polaris* stands in stark contrast to several of Adès's other works, and pushes heavily against his eclectic embrace of techniques in his other large orchestral works such as *Asyla*. Adès's commitment in *Polaris* to thoroughly exploring the consequences of a single kind of surface texture so thoroughly also aligns well with what Adès has described as his fascination with the "play of surfaces."[33] I might speculate that Adès decided

Example 2.6 Adès, *Polaris*, trumpet, mm. 281–330.

to announce *Polaris*'s serialism merely as a fact, information that listeners may or may not choose to incorporate into their experience of the piece. If that is the case, a listener who chooses to do so—who struggles to place this work somehow in conversation with other serialist pieces—is using *Polaris* as a point of departure for his or her own intertextual engagement with the piece. As some of Adès's other works suggest, this may be precisely the point.

Serialism as Surface

Consider the enigmatic opening of Adès's second work for string quartet, *The Four Quarters* (Example 2.7). Its conspicuous dissonance and rhythmic strictness give the feeling of a disciplined style, even on a first hearing. An inspection of the score reveals that not only are all the twelve tones articulated, the first and second violin trade pitches in a strict hocket, piling serialism on top of an isorhythm as well. Even in such a strict texture, Adès subtly breaks

Table 2.1b Adès, *Polaris*, Formal Diagram of End. Lower table continues diagram of the upper one.

	A	B	A	C#	B	A	E	C#	B
Tpt. 1–3	18	23.5	5	21(2)	11(2)	6	22(1)	6	15(3)
Horns 1,3	6	7(2)	4	9(2)	4(7)	3	8(2)	5	8(1)
Tpt. 1–3	0	0	4	6(4)	4(7)	5	6(3)	5	3(5)
Horns 1,3	0	0	4	5(3)	5(5)	4	7(1)	3	4
Tpt. 1–3	5(3)	5	0	3(2)	0	6(2) B3	6(1)	4	0
Tbn 1,2	5	8(2)	3	6(2)	4(6)	4	4(4)	4	9(1)
Horns 1,3	4	6	3	5	7	4	7	2	7
Horns 2,4	4	6	3	5	7	4	7	2	7
Tpt. 1–3	4	6	3	5	7	4	7	2	7
Tbn 1,2	4	6	3	5	7	4	7	2	7
Tuba	4	6	3	5	7	4	7	2	7
	A	G	A	F	G	A	D	F	G

	A	F#	E	C#	B	A	G#	F#	E	C#	B
Tpt. 1-3	0	23	22(2)	7	17(2)	4	18	14	16(2)	8	30(1)
Horns 1,3	0	8	6(2)	6	14(5)	7	11	8	10(8)	3	9(1)
Tpt. 1-3	8	8	6	0	6	3	16	4(2)	6	0	5
Horns 1,3	4	11	3	0	3(1)	4	4(4)	9	3	0	6(9)
Tpt 1-3	9(3) B6	8	4	0	0	8 B5	6	7	9	0	0
Tbn 1,2	0	4	8	2	11(2)	5	5(4)	5	9	3	15
Horns 1,3 (Inv)	0	6	5	3	4	3	9	7	5	3	1
Horns 2,4	0	6	5	3	4	3	9	7	5	3	1
Tpt. 1-3	0	6	5	3	4	3	9	7	5	3	1
Tbn 1,2, 3	0	6	5	3	4	3	9	7	5	3	1
Tba	0	6	5	3	4	3	9	7	5	3	1
	A	C	D	F	G	A	Bb	C	D	F	G

the rules in ways that would only matter to an analyst: in a subsequent statement of the row, he swaps the G and F-sharp while keeping the rest of the row intact. Another sudden moment of serialism occurs at the end of the third movement, "Days," when the first violin suddenly plays an all-combinatorial row, distilling this row from the suggestive trichord figures which precede

Example 2.7 Adès, *The Four Quarters*, "Nightfalls," mm. 1–2. © 2017 Faber Music Ltd, reproduced by kind permission of the publishers.

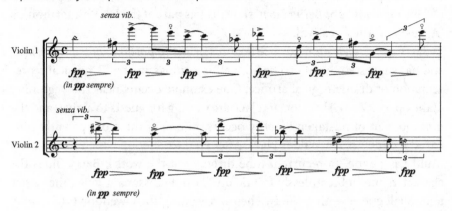

Example 2.8 Adès, *The Four Quarters*, "Days," violin I, ending.

it (Example 2.8). These moments are not the first time Adès has carried out such a turn: as John Roeder has noted, an eleven-note row peeks out near the end of the "Lethe" movement of *Arcadiana*.[34] Neither of these moments, however, provides the obvious structural support that serialism performs in *Polaris*; they convey project a dodecaphonic surface without corresponding architectural underpinnings.

These moments point to the way Adès uses serialism as a surface texture, or what would be called a "topic" in the parlance of musical semiotics. These moments can be freighted with allusive resonances for the listener or analyst who apprehends them, but they remain something of a secret signal given the aforementioned difficulties in aurally grasping a serial moment in an unfolding musical texture. Adès himself has not commented on how we might interpret these moments, but I would argue that we can look to one of his colleagues, Gerald Barry (b. 1952), for a framework to understand some of the affective ends of using tone rows as a surface feature of a work. Adès has long admired the music of Barry, whom he described as his "favorite colleague" in 2011.[35] In 2000, Adès conducted the premiere of Barry's *Wiener Blut*, and between 2002 and 2006 Adès conducted the Birmingham Contemporary Music Group

touring production of one of Barry's most well-known works, his opera
The Triumph of Beauty and Deceit. He also conducted the world premiere
of *The Importance of Being Earnest* in 2011 as part of the LA Philharmonic's
"Aspects of Adès" festival.

Barry uses twelve-tone surface textures in *The Importance of Being Earnest*,
and has suggested that it can be both all-encompassing and a musical repre-
sentation of dramaturgical artifice. One example occurs near the beginning
of the opera, when Algernon and Jack are waiting for guests to arrive (and the
first moment of mistaken identity occurs, in one of the more patently contrived plot devices in Wilde's play). After an introduction which paraphrases
"Auld Lang Syne" (a recurrent tune throughout the work), Barry flings the
characters into a breathlessly frantic duet, wildly dissonant given the rather
tame dialogue of eating sandwiches and waiting for Gwendolyn (Example
2.9). Then, almost as soon as it has started, it is over, and Jack is once again
paraphrasing "Auld Lang Syne."

In a group interview about the work with Adès, Stephen Fry, and Fiona
Shaw, Barry suggests that in this passage he sought to elevate the all-embracing
eclecticism of the drama:

Example 2.9 Gerald Barry, *The Importance of Being* Earnest, mm. 89–95.

GERALD BARRY: I began by writing this very original music. I *mined* myself for this sound, and it sounded fake. There was something about pastiche twelve-tone that seemed more original than my original music. So I use that when Jack and Algernon have their thing about . . .

STEPHEN FRY: "Peculiarly devoted bread and butter."

GB: Yes. So that's all twelve-tone pastiche. But of course, it's a kind of a fine line, because it's the kind of pastiche that, obviously, has to wear well, as well. Then it goes in to all kinds of other music. And there's something about the play—it embraces everything—and so there's all kinds of stuff in it, you know.

FIONA SHAW: I think that's interesting what you're saying now, that it's an icon of construction for the twentieth century.

GB: It contains everything.[36]

In this account, the twelve-tone method is a capacious aesthetic mode that embraces both the eclectic themes of Wilde's play and also the exquisite artifice of the play's narrative devices. Moreover, the actress Fiona Shaw suggests that this eclecticism contributes to the play's iconic status, practically inviting a similarly omnivorous setting for Barry's opera. In his introductory note to the work posted on his publisher's web site, Barry emphasized contrivance rather than eclecticism as the goal of his approach: "Instead of the so-called serial music after the beginning of the opera, I had originally written profound (of course!) music and when I put it together with the text, it sounded fake. And when I substituted the fake serial music, it was true." Barry's theory for why this was satisfying revolved around seeking authenticity through artifice: "Wilde's text is fantastically artificial, and when I went into overdrive to match it with similar originality, it was too heartfelt and became mawkish. It betrayed Wilde's text—making it ordinary. The tension disappeared. When I matched Wilde's artificiality, with highly contrived serialism, both were at home with one another, and there was no false note. One was as fake (artificial) as the other."[37]

Barry's fakeness carries over to a twelve-tone texture that is oddly relaxed. Even a casual glance at the music, which is dominated by the rapid alternation of Jack's and Algernon's vocal lines, reveals that there is no particularly strict handling of the tones. The pitch pattern does repeat every forty-six notes, and all twelve pitch-classes do make an appearance sooner or later. The rhythm is freely deployed, and the instruments, as in *The Triumph of Beauty and Deceit*, mostly provide a jumbled doubling at the octave of the vocal parts, rather than an accompanying texture. On the one hand, this approach could be interpreted as a deliberate flouting of the rules of serialism, instead relying on a shorthand of highly chromatic music with wide octave displacement and *klangfarbenmelodien* in the instrumental accompaniment to convey the impression of a work evocative of the Second Viennese School. On the other hand, Barry may mean he finds *any* kind of compositional approach which smacks of the strictures of twelve-tone technique to be artificial, and therefore ideally expressive for a musical setting of Wilde's play. Considering Adès's own tendency toward eclecticism, and his familiarity with Barry's music, I think Barry's characterization provides one way for considering these moments in *The Four Quarters*.

An important difference between *The Four Quarters* and *The Importance of Being Earnest* is that *The Four Quarters* is instrumental, and so the direct mapping of the serialism into an extrageneric meaning is not so easy; *The Four Quarters* also predates *The Importance of Being Earnest* so it is crucial not to reduce the question to one of mere influence. While it is probably not constructive to try to assign a specific meaning or program to the opening of *The Four Quarters*, it is a moment that entreats us to "politicize the act of listening," as Richard Toop puts it.[38] It is obvious that listeners to Adès's music can extract perfect satisfaction without extensive knowledge of how he interacts with the musical past—it would be hard to account for his broad appeal otherwise. At the same time, listeners who miss these moments are by definition excluded from a certain level of experience of the music. It is hard to ignore serialism's baggage at these moments, when Adès seems to invite Adorno's "expert listener" into a secret elite, not unlike the effect of the hidden virtuosity of Adès's Nancarrow arrangements discussed in the previous essay. While these moments in *The Four Quarters* open up a discursive space for contemplating what an audience ought to be doing, Adès's piano concerto *In Seven Days* seems intent upon using serialism, in concert with other techniques, to prevent even the most sensitive listener from grasping the underlying pattern.

The Serialist Sublime: *In Seven Days*

Adès's piano concerto *In Seven Days* demonstrates yet another facet of his serialism, in which he uses the technique as part of a larger strategy to try to overwhelm the listener's ability to attend to a piece's formal processes. Adès's use of serialist procedures in *In Seven Days* is situated at the far end of the issues of intelligibility, markedness, and salience that seem to form the common thread for his serialist works. The techniques are expanded so far and handled so strictly that they seem to disappear under the weight of their own rigor.

Adès describes *In Seven Days* as a set of variations in which the theme is presented in its simplest form at the end.[39] At its core, the theme is a sequence of twelve chords, with numerous symmetries and tonal implications, and is borrowed from Adès's opera *The Tempest* (Example 2.10).[40] The row used in the third movement, "Land—Grass—Trees," has strong tonal implications of its own, since it is made of alternating major and minor triads (Table 2.2).

Example 2.10 Adès, *In Seven Days*, theme (mvt. vii, rehearsal B). © 2008 Faber Music Ltd, reproduced by kind permission of the publishers.

(015)	(016)	(027)	(015)	(016)	(015)
(0237)	(0126)	(0237)	(0158)	(0157)	(0237)
			Tritone Sub	Tritone Sub	Double Tritone

(0237)	(01358)	(013578)	(013578)	(013578)	(013568)

Table 2.2 *In Seven Days*, Row Matrix

	I_0	I_4	I_9	I_2	I_7	I_{11}	I_3	I_6	I_{10}	I_1	I_8	I_5	
P_0	E	G♯	C♯	F♯	B	D♯	G	B♭	D	F	C	A	R_0
P_8	C	E	A	D	G	B	D♯	F♯	B♭	C♯	G♯	F	R_8
P_3	G	B	E	A	D	F♯	B♭	C♯	F	G♯	D♯	C	R_3
P_{10}	D	F♯	B	E	A	C♯	F	G♯	C	D♯	B♭	G	R_{10}
P_5	A	C♯	F♯	B	E	G♯	C	D♯	G	B♭	F	D	R_5
P_1	F	A	D	G	C	E	G♯	B	D♯	F♯	C♯	B♭	R_1
P_9	C♯	F	B♭	D♯	G♯	C	E	G	B	D	A	F♯	R_9
P_6	B♭	D	G	C	F	A	C♯	E	G♯	B	F♯	D♯	R_6
P_2	F♯	B♭	D♯	G♯	C♯	F	A	C	E	G	D	B	R_2
P_{11}	D♯	G	C	F	B♭	D	F♯	A	C♯	E	B	G♯	R_{11}
P_4	G♯	C	F	B♭	D♯	G	B	D	F♯	A	E	C♯	R_4
P_7	B	D♯	G♯	C♯	F♯	B♭	D	F	A	C	G	E	R_7
	RI_0	RI_4	RI_9	RI_2	RI_7	RI_{11}	RI_3	RI_6	RI_{10}	RI_1	RI_8	RI_5	

Adès has described it as an "organic flowering, the dry land and the trees, a spiraling series. It's a series that can be felt as counterpoint and harmony at the same time . . . an image for organic growth."[41] Any three note subsequence of the row, with the exception of D/F/C, is either a major, minor, augmented, or quintal triad. While there is no simple way to describe the relationship of the row in this movement to the chordal theme of the work overall, the strong tri-adic implications of both allow the work to have a sound which is openly reso-nant and also hints at functional harmony. The gradual rhythmic acceleration of the statement of the rows, combined with their triadic elements, contributes to the overall effect which Adès described as "sort of cell division . . . a slow re-peating thing which always spirals upwards or downwards . . . starting with something huge, like the earth, and then bit by bit it divides, and then you end up with a tiny cell, a blade of grass."[42] Adès's use of biological metaphors in his description of *In Seven Days* engages a larger pattern of serialism intersecting with "rational" modes of composition. In an interview about the piece Adès took as a point of departure the idea that the Book of Genesis served the func-tion of scientific fact at the time it was written.[43] Describing as it does the time before the expulsion from Eden, the work is also utopian, and as such *In Seven Days* reflects a broader trend that Ashby has noticed: that "serialist method-ologies have served as instruments of utopianism, [and] as accessories to a scientistic worldview."[44] Moreover, the visuals provided by Tal Rosner which accompany *In Seven Days* seem to suggest that the third movement is, in its way, the high-water mark of structural considerations and "rationality" in the piece. Rosner's visuals are all taken from either Royal Albert Hall in London or from Disney Hall in Los Angeles, where the work had its double premieres. At the beginning of the third movement, the structural undergirding of Disney Hall becomes the visual subject, a visual parallel to the intricate architecture of Adès's serial processes.

As Adès explained in *Full of Noises*, the statements of the row are elided, so that the final pitch of the first statement of the row becomes the first note of the second. Since the row ends a fifth higher than it begins, all twelve transpo-sitional levels are heard before the original one repeats. This has the ultimate effect of creating a 133-note series, creating an even greater constraint for the pitch material than a twelve-note row. This elided, 133-note row is stated three times, and it is the first hint of both the strictness and the obscurity that Adès embraces in this movement. In the very beginning, the extensive use of suspensions allows the row to unfold slowly, rumbling through the lower ranges of the strings (Example 2.11). In the middle section, Adès expands his use of suspensions, and the winds play descending lines in similar motion,

Example 2.11 Adès, *In Seven Days*, mvt. iii, opening passage.

which, because of the nature of the row, sound tonal but are ultimately a tightly constructed set of voice exchanges (Example 2.12).

In Seven Days has a cosmic ambition, and we might consider the way the piece runs alongside other notions of how the sublime might be conjured in music. While writers on music have considered the "technological" and "cryptographic" sublime for composers as diverse as Nancarrow and Janáček, Adès's use of serialism here is part of a larger effort to overwhelm the listener's critical faculties in order to depict the universe's unfathomable vastness.[45] One might look to the religiously motivated technical innovations of Olivier Messiaen as a precedent for a composer who has used complexity as a means to evoke the divine.[46] Messiaen wrote in his treatise *Technique de mon langage musical* that a listener "will not have time at the concert to inspect the nontranspositions and the nonretrogradations, and at that moment, these questions will not interest him further; to be charmed will be his only desire." But the ultimate effect of Messiaen's language, in his mind, was to engender in the listener's mind a sort of "theological rainbow which the musical language . . . attempts to be."[47] Some of the extraordinarily long durations required for isorhythms to realign in Messiaen's music—for example, in the first movement of the *Quartet for the End of Time*, the cello and piano would take more than 4,100 measures to realign, far longer than the piece itself—have been seen as a musical symbol of everlasting time that Messiaen sought to build in his music; Adès's row-of-rows seems an analogous compositional strategy.

This virtually occluded approach to serialism in *In Seven Days* contrasts starkly with where we began in this essay in our consideration of *Polaris*'s easily understood additive processes. But *In Seven Days* also continues the trend of *The Four Quarters* by using serialism as a programmatic element which helps to create an intricacy so exquisite that it defies a listener who would attend to

Example 2.12 Adès, *In Seven Days*, mvt. iii, suspensions in winds, rehearsal C–D.

Example 2.12 *Continued*

the compositional processes which Adès uses so strictly. Adès's own description of the piece, of attempting to depict the entire universe while simultaneously zooming in to the "cellular" level at other points, suggests that he sought
to stun the listener with a succession of dizzying changes of perspective over
the course of *In Seven Days*. We will return to *In Seven Days* in our discussion
of surrealism in Adès's music; the key point here is that it shows the spectrum
of salience that Adès's serialist works occupy, while also demonstrating how
serialism as a style can perform different functions in his output.

Synthesis and Utopia

It is important not to let serialism mean too much in a portrait of Adès's music.
I would be participating in some of the more problematic aspects of modernist historiography I raised at the beginning of this chapter if I suggested

that Adès's serialist works were somehow a "solution" to a set of "problems" created by his predecessors. Similarly, I am skeptical about the explanatory power of plotting the influences that may have operated on Adès, either via the Second Viennese or Manchester Schools. Put another way, I do not think Adès is a helpless bystander in a web of historical forces, and I cannot abide the view that either the zeitgeist of postmodernism or Adès's subconscious anxiety required him to confront the techniques of the past. The truth probably encompasses all of these factors to some degree, mixed with the inherently multifaceted nature of Adès's own musical sensibility. Nevertheless, we cannot discount the fact that Adès has been quite clear about his use of serialism in some compositions, and it is one of the few techniques—and perhaps the one that is most laden with questions about whether it even matters to audiences or not—that he has specifically drawn attention to in his works. The readings I have provided of serialist works, therefore, are not "exhaustive" because Adès himself does not appear to hold "exhaustion" as a priority in these pieces, and moreover their meanings for us will almost certainly change depending on how Adès decides to use serial techniques in his future works.

I conclude, then, by borrowing from Adès the technique of "zooming out" at the end, to consider how the situation may appear if we take a longer view of composition than the various "-isms" of concert music since the end of the Second World War might initially seem to warrant.[48] The myriad instantiations of serialism in Adès's music show that the technique itself—or rather the set of techniques—does not have a single meaning. As he said of materials in the theme for *In Seven Days*: "They don't mean anything on their own. They're just chords."[49] Similarly, Adès has insisted that style, what he calls the "superficial" qualities of a piece, are meaningless if they don't animate a larger musical effect. In this respect his work is highly idealist, and it is his defense against charges of empty eclecticism.[50]

Adorno proposed in his *Philosophy of Modern Music* that the twelve-tone method as employed by Schoenberg in his late works constituted an unsatisfactory development because it was ultimately dehumanizing—the human subject is in fact enslaved to the compositional process. Adès's uses of serialism dodge this perceived shortcoming. In the pieces considered in this chapter, he asserts his free will in ways ranging from subtle to grandiose, from the swapping of two notes in *The Four Quarters* to the insistent repetition of C-sharp in the material for *Polaris*.

Adès's engagement with serialism invites us to consider his relationship to the earlier twentieth century and that period's own tense compositional dialectic between accessibility and technical innovation. In their way, Adès's serialist works echo themes latent in the growth of serialism in the 1920s and beyond: the method's didactic and polemic quality, its confrontation with what was seen as a stagnating musical culture, its utopian dimensions. Yet Adès's use of serialism also indicates that he has carefully studied the lessons of twentieth-century composers (including those of his fellow countrymen) and refuses to become too invested in a particular technique—be it serialism or, for that matter, serialist pastiche. The constant presence of Adès's own subjectivity in these works—even as, in prose, he insists that he seeks to discover "what the notes want to do"—can be seen as a strong counterweight to the threat of serialism's eradication of human agency.[51] It is this question of human agency, and how it is represented, reconfigured, and sublimated in his opera *The Tempest*, that is the focus of the next essay.

3

The Song Inside Your Mind

The "New Object" of *The Tempest*

Adès's second opera, *The Tempest* (2003), established him as a leading presence in contemporary opera, with productions staged at the Metropolitan Opera, Covent Garden, the Vienna State Opera, and at other venues around the world. In the public imagination, it has solidified comparisons between Adès and Benjamin Britten, the composer of one of the other most well-known Shakespeare operas of the last hundred years, *A Midsummer Night's Dream* (1960). Others have written on Adès's extensive use of interval cycles in *The Tempest*.[1] My focus here is on the larger questions concerning the expressive possibilities of moving from one medium to another and the interpenetration of different frames of reference within the opera.

Adès has had a long-standing fascination with the interpenetration of artworks, both within their own medium (music-to-music) and across multiple media (text-to-music, painting-to-music, and so on). Within Adès's own output, *The Tempest* continues his rich self-borrowing practice discussed in his "glossary" described in Chapter 1. Some of the material in *The Tempest* also appears in the Piano Quintet (2000), *In Seven Days* (2008), and *Lieux Retrouvés* (2009). He has also published related works, including *Scenes from The Tempest* (2004), the overture (2004), and *Court Studies* (2005). In the years following *The Tempest*, he has issued free-standing excerpts or arrangements from all of his operas, releasing *Dances from Powder Her Face* (2007), the *Concert Paraphrase on Powder Her Face* (2009), and *Blanca Variations* (2015). As for the penetration of one art form into another, it is a necessary feature of turning a play into an opera. Adès, however, seeks more than mere replication with music added. He specifically decried Britten's refusal to reimagine *A Midsummer Night's Dream* in *Full of Noises*:

TOM SERVICE: What was your ambition in writing *The Tempest* . . . ? It sets a Shakespeare story, after all, like *A Midsummer Night's Dream*.

ADÈS: I'm absolutely not going to compare myself to Benjamin Britten.

Thomas Adès in Five Essays. Drew Massey, Oxford University Press (2021). © Oxford University Press.
DOI: 10.1093/oso/9780199374960.001.0001.

SERVICE: That's not the point. I'm not asking you to compare yourself to Benjamin Britten. But you just said that it's not ambitious enough to get a speech of Shakespeare and set it to music.

ADÈS: No. I was very specific. I said it would be naff to take a famous passage and set it, verbatim, to a pretty tune. I don't take famous speeches from Shakespeare and put a pretty tune to it, in *The Tempest*. I don't take the famous text at all. It would be half-timbered, mock Tudor, which I find a bit in *A Midsummer Night's Dream*. The music ought to have some reason for existing beyond the fact of us all sitting down and deciding to set this play verbatim to music.[2]

Adès's intensity here reflects the ambitions of his opera and a belief that a more radical transformation is necessary to preserve the spirit of the work's integrity on the operatic stage. Although it will take some time in this essay to hazard an account of *The Tempest*'s "reason for existing," Adès leaves us with little doubt that, in his mind, concordances twixt actor and diva remain mere curiosities without a larger aesthetic agenda.

Adès and Meredith Oakes (*The Tempest*'s librettist) keenly grasped the affective opportunities inherent in the process of transforming Shakespeare's work. Oakes's libretto constitutes a marked departure from Shakespeare's language, swapping out the bard's iambic pentameter for a text that relies on rhyming anapestic couplets. As we will see, this approach elicited a variety of critical responses. In an interview on the occasion of the arrival of the opera in New York in 2012, Adès anticipated criticism of Oakes's libretto, going beyond a defense of her text and offering a deeper aesthetic rationale: "[Critics behaved] as if the play has suddenly disappeared because we've done this . . . The task was not to set the play to music. The task was to make a new object, a different genre, and the rules are very different in opera, because the music has to lead, I think."[3] While any opera based on an existing play is by definition in a "different genre," the "new object" that Adès sought in the creation of *The Tempest* was more of a metamorphosis than merely a transfer of an evening from the theater to the opera house. Adès elaborated on some aspects of this transformation in *Full of Noises*:

When you think of [Shakespeare's *Tempest*], you don't necessarily think of the specific words and speeches, but of the generalized atmosphere that this play produces . . . I could imagine all the composers who have thought about an opera on *The Tempest* . . . sitting down to read the thing, and by the end of Scene 2 they're in despair because it is so apparently formless . . . So I wanted something that would make a geometry from the play, a more right-angled geometry, in two ways: firstly in the language itself, from line to line, and secondly in the plot. I felt, "It won't work if we leave all these unconnected planes, these lacunae in the plot that Shakespeare has." Things that don't really quite make sense, motives that don't quite add up, ends that are left untied, beautiful though they are.[4]

Adès's comments, with their emphasis on the overall spirit of the play and its contour in a composer's imagination, point to a goal which might be more accurately described as *conjuring* Shakespeare's *Tempest* rather than *reciting* it. From this perspective, critics' quick disdain for the libretto originates in a failure to grasp the peculiar challenges confronting an operatic team working to materialize *The Tempest*. As Adès indicates, and as we will see ourselves, there is more going on in Oakes's libretto than merely streamlining the opera, or making it "easier to understand" as Oakes and Adès gamely proposed was the purpose of their textual interventions in a 2012 interview.[5] A closer look at the opera reveals that they sought a wholesale reimagining of *The Tempest* for the medium of opera, and Oakes's libretto sits at the core of that effort.

Adès's and Oakes's decision to push past the confines of Shakespeare's language in search of a different, more musical truth reflects another priority of Adès's that is relevant here. Adès has ruminated about how liberation of music from generic classification can lead to the dissolution of the boundary between creator and listener. As he explained in a 2011 interview:

I avoid those labels and boxes, but eventually you're going to be put in some kind of box. It's like my fear of being buried alive. You are who you are—that comes first, rather than any particular style. I think it's more important to me that when you put it on, it's live and alive. It goes straight into the listener, absorbs them, in a way. I like that feeling that you're not sitting on one side of a glass wall and the music is on the other side. When I have a great experience with a piece of music, I get the feeling that it's happening in my own brain—in me, rather than on the stage. I want to get inside you, so that you feel like it's going on in your mind. I don't mean for it to sound creepy! It's a nice thing. That's what the best music does to me.[6]

In the context of his *Tempest*, Adès's remarks here take on an especially sharp edge. In particular, this line of thinking proceeds directly from avoiding preconceived mental models to creating a metaphorically penetrative experience between composer and listener. This melting of subjectivity, predicated on a disregard for the niceties of generic, historical, and stylistic boundaries, is especially evident in Adès's and Oakes's treatment of Ariel, and is precisely the beachhead on which we will land for our tour of Adès's version of Prospero's island.

Borrowed Words and the Enigma of Ariel

Britten and Pears cleaved closely to the original and introduced only a single new line of text in their entire libretto of *A Midsummer Night's Dream*, but one of the most immediately striking features of Oakes's libretto is its fresh rhyming couplets.[7] For example, Ariel's famous song to Ferdinand is re-imagined:

Shakespeare	Oakes
Full fathom five thy father lies.	Five fathoms deep
Of his bones are coral made.	Your father lies
Those are pearls that were his eyes.	Those are pearls
Nothing of him that doth fade	That were his eyes
But doth suffer a sea change	Nothing of him
Into something rich and strange.	That is mortal
Sea nymphs hourly ring his knell.	Is the same
(1.2.474–480)	His bones are coral
	He has suffered
	A sea change
	Into something
	Rich and strange
	Sea nymphs hourly
	Ring his knell
	(1.5.R90–93)[8]

Critical reactions to this strategy were mixed. *The Economist* found the libretto "witty and concise."[9] Zachary Woolfe wrote in the *Observer*, "there are ineptly rhyming couplets like 'Fearful story/I'm so sorry,' and an antiqued, ersatz mood that feels out of step with the score. Mr. Adès's work has classical inspirations and aspirations, but it is of our time, seething and strange. It deserves less polite, less stagnant words."[10]

If it was these couplets which attracted so much attention, perhaps more interesting are the ways in which Oakes's libretto reconfigures the narrative mechanics of the story to create what might be called a kind of "citational" approach to its structure (Table 3.1). Oakes's couplets may here be considered merely the surface of her strategy, whereas the volume may be located in the manner in which the libretto not only truncates Shakespeare's original but also leaps through it, shuttling back and forth through the play as well as the play's long historical shadow. This approach is important because it establishes that the integrity of the characters ultimately rests somewhere outside of the

Table 3.1 Shakespeare/Oakes Concordance for *Tempest*

Shakespeare	Characters	Notes	Oakes	Characters	Notes
1.1	Master and Boatswain; then Mariners; then Alonso, Sebastian, Antonio, Ferdinand, Gonzalo, and Court	Not concordant	1.1	Court (Offstage)	Chorus Quotes Ariel 1.2.252–53 (hell is empty)
1.2	Propsero and Miranda;	1.2.1–223	1.2	Miranda and Prospero	
	then Ariel;	1.2.224–362; (1.2.363–84 transition)	1.3	Ariel and Prospero	1.2.224–65
	then Caliban;	1.2.385–451 (Miranda Awake)	1.4	Caliban & Prospero (Miranda Asleep)	
			1.5	Prospero & Ariel (Miranda Asleep)	1.2.266–1.2.355 & 1.2.474–82 (Full fathom five)
	then Ferdinand.	1.2.483–618	1.6	Ferdinand & Miranda (Prospero and Ariel Unseen)	Ariel sings "bow wow" from earlier, 1.2.459;
2.1	Alonso, Sebastian, Antonio, Gonzalo, Adrian, Francisco, and court; then Ariel (invisible)	Antonio and Sebastian murder subplot (2.1.208–2.1.377) moved later in Oakes.	2.1	Court, Stefano, Trinculo, Antonio, Sebastian, Gonzalo, and the King (Prospero and Ariel Unseen)	R119–R125: Court portrays Gonzalo's amazement at their unscathed clothes (from 2.1.64ff.) (Both first and second act open with choral numbers); R125–26: Introduces Trinculo and Stefano (drunk already; ahead of 2.2) R127: Choral Echo R128–30: Prospero & Ariel, presumably acting out the implied commands following 1.2.600 (never spoken). Note here that rhythm and rhyme matches Stephano's "wrong" version of Ariel's song at 3.2.133–35.

		R130–34: Consoling King (op. cit: 2.1.104–2.1.207) R134–50: Ariel sows discontent; see 3.2.46–166 (although there she ventriloquizes Trinculo to Stephano, not Sebastian to Antonio and vice versa).
2.2	Caliban;	As before, with Caliban The court never sees Caliban in Shakespeare (at least not yet). R150–65: covers action 2.2.1–194 (i.e., the full scene), with incidental text from the court, who now watch as Stephano and Trinculo drink with Taliban. R166: Ariel picks up the tune that the court and Caliban is singing; point back to 3.2.138. R170: Full of Noises Aria; in this context a hymn to music itself, rather than the ravings of a drunk savage. R174: Gonzolo (addressing Caliban as "sir") asks for his help to find Ferdinand. Caliban recapitulates the sentiment, if not the action, of his speech to Prospero 1.2.395–411. R181–88: largely new, since Antonio, Caliban, and Propsero are never on the stage together until the end of Shakespeare's original; Conflates 3.3.114–32 (where Antonio figures out that Prospero is on the island, from Ariel's "Harpy" speech. R190: Sebastian berates Antonio. R191–94: Court resolves to find Ferdinand; King remains bereft. R195: Prospero, appearing after departure, gloats over the court's confusion.
	then Trinculo; then Stephano	

Continued

Table 3.1 Continued

Shakespeare	Characters	Notes	Oakes	Characters	Notes
			2.3	Caliban, Stefano, Trinculo	Plot to kill Prospero, so that Stefano can marry Miranda. Carries out the action of 3.2.46–166.
3.1	Ferdinand; then Miranda and Prospero (P. unseen)		2.4	Ferdinand; then Miranda; then Prospero (Unseen)	Accurate concordance, except for the operatic convenience that Miranda frees Ferdinand rather than having him somehow wriggle out between Act 1 and here (as is the case in Shakespeare). Harmonic language at R220 anticipates more extended form in passacaglia duet.
3.2	Caliban, Stephano, and Trinculo; then Ariel (unseen)		3.1	Caliban, Stefano, Trinculo	The trio continues to scheme, and is still drunk. Essentially recapitulates the action of 2.3 in the opera, and 3.2 in the play.
3.3	Alonso, Sebastian, Antonio, Gonzalo, Adrian, Francisco, "etc."; then Prospero (unseen); then "several strange shapes"; then Ariel, "like a Harpy"	Banquet Masque	3.2	Prospero and Ariel, then Court	R241–245: Prospero and Ariel Dialogue has no clear concordance (5.1.1–66?) R246–53: 3.3.1–10 R253–57: Antonio and Sebastian Murder Subplot (while the court sleeps, 2.1.208–2.1.377) compressed here. R258: Ariel wakes court (supplanting the "Harpy" soliloquy 3.3.70–101). R259–60: Gonzalo confronts Antonio and Sebastian (drawn) (3.3.114–33). Although in play, they exit to seek Propsero, here the banquet masque immediately follows. (3.3.25–69) R270–73: "Men of Sin" Speech again; (3.3.70–101) R274–78: King & Antonio finally realize that Prospero is on the island, and now they properly exit to hunt Prospero (3.3.120). R279: "Boil'd in thy skull" speech, 5.1.67–97; although in terms of the action of the play this speech happens at the moment that Prospero decides to forgive the court.

4.1	Prospero, Ferdinand, and Miranda; then Ariel; then Iris; then Ceres; then Juno; then Nymphs; then Reapers; then Caliban, Stephano, and Trinculo; then "divers spirits"	Iris Masque	3.3	Miranda, Ferdinand, and Prospero; then Calbian, Stefano, and Trinculo	R283–84: 4.1.1–36. R285: Ferdinand sees Ariel (not in play until after masque). R286: Masque (4.1.67–130). Truncated, and reveals that Alonso is alive (doesn't happen until 5.1.210; instead he and Miranda repair to Prospero's house in the play). R290: "Our revels are ended" 4.1.165–80 (such stuff that dreams are made on speech) R293–301: 4.1.218–95 Caliban with Stefan and Trinculo, although Prospero summons hounds in the play and immobilizes and makes them disappear in the opera (after a direct confrontation). R302–05: 5.1.9–40.
5.1	Prospero and Ariel; then Alonso, Gonzalo, Sebastian, Antonio, Adrian, and Francisco; then Miranda and Ferdinand; then Ariel (with Master and Boatswain); then Ariel (with Caliban, Stephano, and Trinculo)		3.4	Everyone (eventually), except Caliban	R306–08: 5.1.114–31; opera skips forward to: R309–11: 5.1.205–14 R311–14: Passacaglia 5.1.215-8 R315: 5.1.360 (Prospero indicates ship; in play Boatswain returns). R317: O Brave new world R318–21: 5.1.293–367 (Stephano and Trinculo return, although in the play, unlike in the opera, Caliban does *not* come onstage. R323–4: Prospero paraphrasing 5.1.149–54 R323–24: Antonio's "you'll forgive at no cost" echoes the sentiment of Auden. R325: 5.1.63–66 R326: Prospero breaks his staff: quotes Auden, "Stay with me Ariel"
			3.5	Caliban, with Ariel Offstage	Op. cit Auden, *The Sea and the Mirror.* Mirrors Caliban's monologue (half to himself); and then the final section, Ariel's echo, with only the word " . . . I"
Epilogue	Prospero	Not concordant			

libretto, and moreover deconstructs the integrity of the imagined self (or what Adès called the "psychology") of the characters. In Oakes's hands, the aggregate effect of this approach is not so much a random reading of Shakespeare, but a gradual disintegration of certain characters—especially Ariel—as fully drawn individuals, allowing them instead to serve a number of purposes in Adès's "new object."

The first scene in the opera provides a good example of this aspect of Oakes's writing. As the curtain rises, the orchestra and staging carry the responsibility of depicting the eponymous tempest in an extended instrumental introduction until the last sixteen bars, when the chorus sings "Hell is empty / All the devils are here." In Shakespeare, the phrase "Hell is empty" appears in Ariel's account of forcing the court ashore that he gives to Prospero in Act 1, Scene 2:[11]

> All but Mariners
> Plunged in the foaming brine and quit the vessel,
> Then all afire with me. The King's son, Ferdinand,
> With hair up-staring—then like reeds, not hair—
> Was the first man that leaped; cried "Hell is empty
> And all the devils are here." (1.2.248–53)

It may seem a minor point that the chorus sings a phrase that is actually Ferdinand's, which we only hear in Shakespeare's play as quoted by Ariel in a speech to Prospero. After all, the chorus ought to sing *something*. The reason it is germane here is that the opera opens by announcing its own departure from any literal concordance between itself and Shakespeare's play. More subtly, Oakes's libretto also immediately destabilizes our certainty about who is speaking when the chorus sings. It is neither Ariel (the agent of the chaos) nor Ferdinand (reliant as the plot is on the fact that he is separated from his fellow floaters). The text is plucked from Shakespeare's original without need for fidelity to its original context; in this way Oakes signals to the audience that this will be an opera that exalts in playing with the structure of the original, using it as a fund of imagery as much as a basis for the plot.

Although it is Oakes's chorus that first steals words out of the mouths of others, Oakes's Ariel seems to be the best at it. The final scene of Act 1 closes with vocal pyrotechnics by Ariel, responding to Prospero's instructions to bring the court to him (Example 3.1). "Bow wow" is Ariel's recurrent text here as the curtain falls. In Shakespeare's play, however, Ariel sings this line not at the end of a scene, but to calm Ferdinand in Act 1, Scene 2. Although Ferdinand tells us that "This music crept by me upon the waters, allaying both their fury and my passion with its sweet air," (1.2.469–71) Adès's setting,

Example 3.1 Adès, *The Tempest*, Act 1, Scene 6, R117 to end. "The Tempest" by Thomas Adès and Meredith Oakes, © 2007 Faber Music Ltd, reproduced by kind permission of the publishers.

Example 3.1 *Continued*

with its wildly disjunct leaps and shrill register, is anything but soothing. Furthermore, it isn't clear that Ariel sings this line at all in the original. Shakespeare's stage directions for the text "bow-wow" reads: "Burden dispersedly, within"—indicating that it is instead an offstage chorus, singing heterophonically or at least antiphonally, that should deliver this line in the play rather than Ariel himself. In other words, although the chorus began by quoting Ariel (himself quoting Ferdinand), now Adès's Ariel has usurped the role of Shakespeare's chorus.

Just as Adès thrills to hear another's music as though it was "happening in my own brain," Oakes's version of Ariel has absorbed other *Tempest* characters so fully that he speaks their words as though his own. Ariel's citational trickery continues in the first scene of Oakes's second act. Prospero and Ariel, unseen, surveil the stupefied court. In this passage, Ariel's and Prospero's lines do not correspond to any of theirs in Shakespeare's original. Instead, the two paraphrase the moment in Shakespeare's third act in which Caliban, Stephano, and Trinculo sing a little catch (or round), giddy at having planned Prospero's murder:[12]

Shakespeare	Oakes
STEPHANO (*sings*): Flout 'em and scout 'em And scout 'em and flout 'em! Thought is free. CALIBAN: That's not the tune. *Ariel plays the tune on a tabor and pipe.* STEPHANO: What is this same? TRINCULO: This is the tune of our catch played by the picture of Nobody. (3.2.133–6)	ARIEL & PROSPERO: Taunt them, haunt them, goad and tease. Prick them, tick them, give no peace. (2.1.R129)

Adès's setting of Oakes's text here underscores the paraphrase, placing Prospero and Ariel in the rough imitative texture of a country round, like two singers who don't quite know their own part (Example 3.2). Ariel continues to plagiarize other characters later in the same scene by Oakes, for example when he speaks in the voice of Antonio and Sebastian in order to continue to sow discontent among members of the court (Example 3.3). In Shakespeare's play, Ariel's ventriloquism is a device particular to Act 3, Scene 2, when Ariel impersonates Trinculo to Stephano and Caliban (3.2.69–84). Oakes's decision to have Ariel (and, to a lesser extent, Prospero) leap forward in the play to reference a later scene suggests a kind of omniscience on the part of the characters, as if Oakes's Ariel has a copy of Shakespeare's *Tempest* sitting on his nightstand and spends lazy afternoons flipping through it to find the best bits and get to them before someone else does.

Oakes's characters have not merely internalized Shakespeare; her ending gazes beyond Shakespeare's own words, toward the citational world of W. H. Auden's *The Sea and the Mirror* (1942–44). Auden described this sprawling five part work—part poem, part prose—as a "Commentary on Shakespeare's *The Tempest*," and it imagines a hypothetical future for the characters beyond the end of the play. Auden's work splinters in multiple directions; broadly speaking, Oakes has picked up on the aspects which further enrich the depths of the characters. Oakes only directly quotes Auden once: when Prospero implores Ariel, "stay with me," suggesting a tenderness and vulnerability on Prospero's part that Shakespeare's matter-of-fact conclusion lacks. This single direct quotation reflects a more thoroughgoing commitment to augment Shakespeare's characters. For example, Antonio has only one incidental line in the final scene of Shakespeare. Oakes, by contrast, includes

Example 3.2 Adès, *The Tempest*, Act 2, Scene 1, R129.

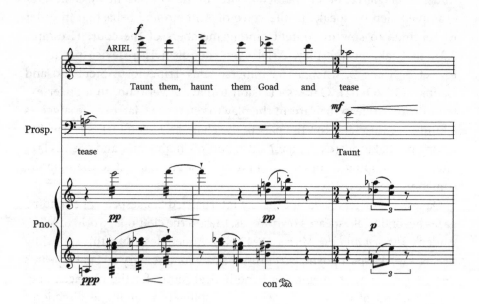

Example 3.3 Adès, *The Tempest*, Act 2, Scene 1, R134–5 to R134+1.

a bitter arioso by Antonio, which recapitulates the brooding sour grapes of Auden's Antonio:[13]

Auden	Oakes
Antonio, sweet brother, has to laugh.	ANTONIO
How easy you have made it to refuse	You'll forgive at no cost
Peace to your greatness! Break your wand in half,	You've won, I've lost.
	I've lost my pride my life
The fragments will join; burn your books or lose	Your child is Naples wife.
Them in the sea, they will soon reappear,	Naples wife, spoiled child of fortune
Not even damaged: as long as I choose	Which you call the will of heaven.
	The will of heaven which decreed
To wear my fashion, whatever you wear	You were born better than me.
Is a magic robe; while I stand outside	Better than me with my poor courage
Your circle, the will to charm is still there.	Which has turned to your advantage
	Your advantage blocks my breath
	And your life has been my death.

At the end of Auden's monologue for Antonio, the deposed usurper forcefully asserts his selfhood:

> *Your all is partial, Prospero;*
> *My will is all my own:*
> *Your need to love shall never know*
> *Me: I am I, Antonio,*
> *By choice myself alone.*[14]

Antonio's insistence on his sovereignty as an individual grates against the broader, dreamlike atmosphere of *The Tempest*. For Auden, this assertion of selfhood also contributes to the overall effect of the longest portion of *The Sea and The Mirror*, in which Caliban speaks directly to the audience. In Auden's version, Caliban is endowed with extraordinary rhetorical power, delivering a faux-learned discursus which begins with a cathartic sneer at the now-departed Prospero. Caliban continues through a series of imagined futures for the other characters, as breathless as a man with a pent-up need to be heard who has therefore written a speech far too long for the allotted time. Auden's Caliban finishes with an assertion of his own irreducible existence, and the folly of the play's effort. At this point, Auden's Caliban appears to take his own citational turn, more closely approximating Puck's sentiment at the end of *A Midsummer Night's Dream* than Prospero's at the end of *Tempest*: "Now it is over. No, we have not dreamt it. Here we really stand, down stage with red faces

and no applause; no effect, however simple, no piece of business, however un-
important, came off."[15] The character's seeming awareness of their own unre-
ality obtains in the opera too: Oakes's Caliban states his own name, apparently
sure of that, but skeptical that anything else he has seen is real, losing his train
of thought so totally that he even drops the rhyming scheme in his closing line:

> Who was here
> Have they disappeared?
> Were there others?
> Were we brothers?
> Did we feast? And give gifts?
> Were there fires? And ships?
>
> They were human seeming
> I was dreaming
> In the gleam of the sand
> Caliban
> In the hiss of the spray
> In the deep of the bay
> In the gulf in the swell
> Caliban

Oakes's incidental references to Auden might remain a curiosity if they
didn't point to an effort on the part of both authors to reconsider the subjective reality of Ariel as well. In Shakespeare, Ariel is freed moments before
Prospero's closing monologue and heard from no more. In Auden, however,
Ariel provides a rejoinder to Caliban at the end of Auden's proem:

> Tempt not your sworn comrade,—only
> As I am can I
> Love you as you are—
> For my company be lonely
> For my health be ill:
> I will sing if you will cry
>
>   ... I
>
> [...]
>
> This was long ago decided,
> Both of us know why,
> Can, alas foretell,

> When our falsehoods are divided,
>   What we shall become,
>   One evaporating sigh
>   . . . /[16]

Ariel is an extension of Prospero's will in the play; Auden's closing stanzas
upend this dynamic. For Auden, there is a self for Ariel, an "I" that was always
there but exerted no independent agency until manumission (Auden tells
us the "I" in this passage is an "Echo by the PROMPTER"). This fact becomes
central to Oakes's ending, which reconfigures the relative emphasis of the
different storylines as the work draws to a close. The opera ends with a disem-
bodied and liberated Ariel singing offstage, and Caliban alone on the island
(Example 3.4). Both have been apparently restored to selfhood: Caliban sings
his name and the virtues of the island. Ariel sings only his name, yet in gaining
his freedom has apparently lost the ability to form consonants: his final lines
only read "A-i-e," with the instruction "use vowels from word 'Ariel' to end."
He has become, true to Auden, "one evaporating sigh," unseen like Auden's
prompter.

Ariel's fluent plagiarism in Oakes's libretto might be interpreted as a reflection of the fact that he is an emanation of Prospero's agency until the very end.
Although in many respects Ariel is one of the most striking presences in the
opera—the stratospheric *fach* of Adès's writing makes sure of that—he spends

Example 3.4 Adès, *The Tempest*, Act 3, Scene 5, R330 to R330+4.

* Use vowels from word "Ariel" to end

most of the play obeying Prospero. Even after liberation, Oakes's Ariel still can't quite fit his lips around his own name—Auden at least allows Ariel an "I" at the end, even if only echoed. If we return to Adès's imagery of music that lives inside the listener, we can summarize by way of analogy. Shakespeare, and the penumbra of Shakespeare, live inside of Ariel, but a separate free-standing dramaturgical agent does not.[17] Put another way, Ariel's enigma is simply this: Ariel is both one of the central characters of Adès's *Tempest*, and not really a character at all. One path through this contradiction is to accept that Ariel was never intended to represent an individual: instead, it is precisely Ariel's lack of self that allows the music to step in and convey its own mysterious charms.

Adès's "Layers of Desire"

The evaporation of Ariel at the precise moment when he is finally free points to Adès's boldest strategy in *The Tempest*: the characters aren't represented *by* the music, they *are* the music. We can be sure of Adès's commitment to this approach because he has said as much in *Full of Noises*:

SERVICE: In *The Tempest*, with all those materials moving in different directions—if the notes have their own will, do the individual characters have will too?

ADÈS: Well, the characters don't exist without the material: when I say characters I'm talking about fifteen separate tendencies in the material, which are more or less related.[18]

This kind of conceptualization for the overall organization of *The Tempest* is arguably inherent in the original Shakespeare. Ian Bostridge noted that the play pointed strongly toward a different approach than simply "setting" the text for the opera:

An opera based on *The Tempest* would be something . . . growing out of its central musical metaphor and the quintessentially Renaissance idea of music itself as a form of sympathetic magic. Shakespeare's island hums with music; but the play uses music for its own theatrical purposes. An opera would have to make a new *Tempest* out of musical materials that have their own logic.[19]

Adès, too, underscored the idea of music that possesses its own interior agency. "The aim," he explained with regard to *The Tempest*, "was essentially to write a symphonic opera, which means that in theory the evening is driven by the musical logic at least as much as by the logic of the drama itself."[20] The question that both Adès and Bostridge are addressing here is how to root the aesthetic coherence of an opera based on *The Tempest*. A reliance on "logic" is not necessarily a foregone conclusion for an Adès opera—consider the kaleidoscopic narrative and musical styles of *Powder Her Face* or the absurdist dimensions of *The Exterminating Angel*. In the case of *The Tempest*, however, the belief in an autonomous musical force at the center of the opera loomed so strongly in the symbolic order that everything, and everyone, became subordinate to it in Adès's mind. When Tom Service asked Adès about whether he or Oakes chose the "overall shape of the opera," Adès replied: "The music decided, really."[21]

Adès made a historical argument for why *The Tempest* required an approach in which the music is not just dominant but seems endowed with its own life force. His efforts to characterize a "symphonic opera" in *Full of Noises* center on his assessment of Wagner's shortcomings and Berlioz's successes:

> Good symphonies are often in some ways an unfolding sequence of miniatures. They have to go through miniature forms as they go along, and what bothers me with Wagner's music is that there's a pretense of some kind of symphonic thought when there actually isn't any, where none is possible because he can't trust himself . . . Berlioz, in *Les Troyens*, is much more successful to me. In that opera, you are clear that there are numbers, there are actors in a drama, and that something is happening . . . We are taking part in a symphonic event in which specific things are happening and they are woven into a music which is in itself dramatically alive.[22]

Lest there be any doubt about Adès's estimation of the cost that Wagner paid for his approach, Adès made a further distinction between musical logic and other possible modes of organization:

> In Wagner the logic is philosophical or psychological. It's not a musical logic . . . You see, to me, notes are like angels, they are innocent at the point of origin. But the moment Wagner writes a note it is forced to stand for something extra-musical . . . In Wagner every note is political and that to me is repulsive.[23]

Even on its own, the absolute primacy of music in Adès's ambitions for *The Tempest* begins to make clear some of the priorities in the arrangement of the libretto: borrowings, citations, rearrangements, and paraphrases are all consistent with a stance that insists that the music's will is pure, and that all other dimensions of the work—perhaps the text in particular—must obey it in order to preserve the opera's integrity.

If we turn to the score of *The Tempest* to see how this approach manifests in practice, the first scene of Act 2 proves particularly revealing. Adès described the material of *The Tempest* as being made of "layers of desire" that endow the composition with its own self-activated destiny:

> There will always be some unfolding process in any piece, but in an opera it could go anywhere, because instead of having two or three or four layers of desire, as you might have in a piano piece, there might be, say, fifteen . . . You might have so many, in fact, that you're not sure who . . . is going to win. I know what happens to the characters on stage in the story, but I don't know how that functions in the music until it's composed.[24]

Adès later made a further distinction that these tendencies ought to stand apart from the composer, hence reflecting an autonomous musical logic, elaborating on his disdain for Wagner:

> I'm more interested in an art where you can see the different elements in a clear glass jar . . . In that case, the magic is even more powerful, more mysterious, because you can clearly see the elements that create this indefinable magic as separate entities . . . If everything [in an opera] is connected, developed together—fused in a Wagnerian chemical concoction—then we don't have characters, really. All the characters are only facets of the same person, who is actually the creator of the opera. So in Wagner all the characters are aspects of Wagner.[25]

Nowhere is the independence of the characters in *The Tempest* on more ample display than in this scene, which depicts the court as it finds itself alive but shipwrecked on Prospero's island. The characters swiftly move through a series of miniatures in the style of an eighteenth-century dance suite (Table 3.2). As if to underscore the independence of characters, this is the only scene in the opera that features explicit key signatures: Adès places Antonio and Sebastian at opposite key centers of D and A-flat major, musically portraying characters who can't seem to inhabit the same tonal world (these two keys, being separated by a tritone, share only two pitches—G and C-sharp/D-flat—in their respective diatonic collections). Adès does not give any of his tendencies specific names, but this scene makes clear that both tonal grounding through a key signature and neo-Baroque gestural language are fundamental features of Adès's material for the court. Other characters use highly demarcated melodic styles as well. Although not well represented in this scene, Prospero's melodies in *The Tempest* tend to orbit around a gesture that includes a small step and then a larger leap.[26] The King's few lines almost

Table 3.2 Selected "Tendencies" in *The Tempest*. Final row indicates works written after *The Tempest* in which the tendencies recur.

Piano Quintet, mm. 1–16	Six Chords	Liberation	"Fetish" Note (Ariel's high E)	Baroque (also tendency to inhabit a specific key signature)	Wagner Slice	Melisma
1.2.R15 (Accompaniment)						
1.2.R36 (Miranda)						
1.2.R85 (Ariel)	1.5.92 (Ariel)		1.3.R44			
			1.5.R90			
1.6.R94+3 (Ferdinand)						
1.6.R105+3 (Ferdinand)			1.6.R118 (end of act)			
2.1.R142 (Antonio)				2.1.R131: Prelude 2.1.R133: Courante (D) 2.1.R137: Branle (A-flat) 2.1.R138: Louré / Fanfare (D) 2.1.R141: Lament (B) 2.1.R146: Fanfare (D)		2.1.R126 (Stephano and Trinculo – "Smooth")
		2.2.R167 (Ariel)			2.2.R170: Caliban (A = Earth)	2.2.R167 (Ariel)
	2.1.R193 (King's Grief)					
2.4.R224		2.4.R220 (Miranda and Ferdinand)				

Lieux Retrouvés, ii.	Court Studies	Court Studies, In Seven Days, mm. 142-154.
		2.4.R226 Prospero (Inverted)
		3.1.1 (Orchestra)
3.2.R249		
	3.2.R261 (Banquet: Orchestra ventriloquizes Ariel's passage from end of Act 1)	
3.2.R264+5		
	3.2.R266: Gonzalo (C – People)	
	3.2.R271-2 (Harpy Aria)	
	3.2.R273 (Harpy Liquidation)	
3.2.R287 (Masque; as accompaniment at 1.2.R15)		
		3.4.R305+4
3.4.R306 (Hymn / Chaccone)	3.4.R306: Chaccone (no notated key: C)	
		3.4.R319
	3.4.R323: Gavotte	3.4.321 (Chorus)
		3.4.R326 (Ariel)
		3.4.R327 (Prospero Inverted)
		3.4.R328 (Caliban)
	3.4.R332 (Ariel, freed)	
	3.4.R333 (pianissimo)	

all feature a gradually descending chromatic line; the Prince and the "False Duke" both are represented by neo-Baroque figurations which, in their way, echo Adès's fascination with Couperin.

The characters not only have distinct styles; Adès has written a free-standing instrumental work, *Court Studies* (2005), which is derived from this scene and which highlights the "layers of desire" that apply to the court and underscore their qualities as purely musical entities. As its name implies, *Court Studies* is a short chamber suite based on the music of the court from *The Tempest* for clarinet, violin, cello, and piano. *Court Studies* focuses on the portrayal of each musical character, however, rather than constructing a narrative parallel to the opera. This choice is most evident in Adès's decision to title the sections according to the names of characters from the opera (Table 3.3). Although the work lacks the textual point of reference of Meredith Oakes's libretto, it can also be argued that this is a stripping-away of extraneous material in Adès's mind, in order to present the unadulterated musical substance of the characters themselves. In its way, *Court Studies* provides a map for the styles

Table 3.3 *Court Studies* Concordance

Court Studies Name / mm.	Scene	Tempest Rehearsal & Incipit
Fanfare / 1–3	2/1	R 146 Chorus: "It's all his fault / and still he talks" Or Antonio: "I don't deserve / your hurtful words"
"The False Duke" / 4–29	2/1	R 133–34; 135–36 "Sir I saw him / I saw him in the water"; "Sir the tempest has not claimed him"
"The Prince" / 30–65	2/1	R 137–40 "Milan your vanity / your self promotion Have brought us to this god forsaken short"
"The King" / 66–83	2/1	R 141 (ends before 142) "Oh prince of Naples and Milan / What fish has made its meal on you!"
"The False Duke's Defeat" / 84–117	3/4	R 323–25 "You'll forgive / at no cost "You've won / I've lost"
Fanfare / 115–17	2/1	R 146
"Counsellor" / 118–41	2/1	R 131–3 before 133 "Sir be cheerful "This is remarkable!"
"The King's Grief" / 143–54	2/1	R 193–94+1 "The sea mocks / Our search on land "He's lost / Whom we stray to find"

which the characters inhabit in the second act, and as such serves as a contin-uation or working out of Adès's thoughts on portraying characters musically in opera, in a manner which lends each character a sovereign patch of musical terrain.

While the music relating to the court characters has strong generic markers, Adès has also gone so far as to concentrate these musically autonomous structures into a single note. Adès has called these individual notes which carry a musical work forward "fetish notes:"

> It's something in the way I hear all music, actually, this idea of there being a single note—a particular pitch on a particular instrument—that has a crucial function across whole structures. It's an analytical thing that I don't find reflected in written analysis enough, and it's something that I really feel is important. It's the idea of a fetish note in a piece: that certain specific pitches become fetish objects, which are returned to and rubbed by the composer all the time. It doesn't matter what key we're in, or what's happening around it in terms of the context of the music—that note on that instrument.[27]

Adès provides the example of the F in the first violin at the beginning of the Piano Quintet as a fetish; Ariel's high E also fits his description. This pitch occurs at several structurally significant points: Ariel's first entrance, the end of the first act, and the end of the opera overall. Moreover, when Ariel "plays soft music" for the court during the banquet scene, the orchestra ventriloquizes his closing aria from the first act, replete with a high E sounding as Ariel remains mute (Example 3.5). Adès's writing for the island spirit has become notorious for its difficulty, calling for more than seventeen high Es in his first passage, and encompassing an extraordinary range, from the A-flat below middle C to the G above the staff.[28] In an interview with David Weininger from 2011, Adès seemed to consider Ariel's tessitura integral to the success of the opera, and underscored its pathology and risk: "I don't really know if anyone can do this, but I'm completely sure that it's what has to happen at this point. So if it's not possible, the whole subject of 'The Tempest' isn't possible for me . . . I just hope that if it comes down onto the page and I know it's theoretically possible, then it is right. And I hope to just sort of stand my ground when the time comes and to say, you know, keep going."[29] Ariel's entrance aria, and indeed his per-formance throughout the first act, has become a signal feature of the opera, standing alongside the Duchess's notorious aria from *Powder Her Face* as a signal moment in Adès's writing for voice.

Although the first scene of the second act may provide the clearest ex-ample of Adès's "tendencies," we find them throughout *The Tempest*, for

Example 3.5 Adès, *The Tempest*, Act 1, Scene 3, R44 to R44+5; Adès, *The Tempest*, Act 3, Scene 2, R261 to R261+5.

example in the passacaglia which opens Act 3, Scene 4. This scene also points at how different tendencies can converge at crucial moments. Here, Miranda and Ferdinand are reunited with the court. As a passacaglia, this section's allusion to eighteenth-century forms encountered at the beginning of the second act is unmistakable. The section also borrows the harmonic language from another tendency, the harmonic feints which Adès identifies as originating in the Piano Quintet and looming throughout the opera.[30] Adès explained in *Full of Noises* that this particular sequence started as a second piano quintet, but was transformed. "Instead of being concerned with time and movement in a horizontal sense, this was concerned with vertical space . . . So of course to the outside ear it couldn't be more different from the world of the Piano Quintet, but it is the same material and that's where it started."[31]

Adès's comment also points to another element of these "layers of desire," namely that they span other works and can mean many things. For example, the six chords which accompany Ariel at the end of his "Five Fathoms Deep" aria also appear in Adès's piano concerto *In Seven Days*. When Adès pointed this out in *Full of Noises*, his interlocutor Tom Service gamely served up the question "Do they mean the same thing in the opera and in *In Seven Days*?" to which Adès scoffed: "No. They don't mean anything, on their own, they're just chords."[32] But then, having apparently dismissed them as "just chords," Adès makes a characteristic reversal and argues the opposite:

SERVICE: But aren't they different objects because of the different situations you press them into service for?

ADÈS: They're not a leitmotif.

SERVICE: I don't mean they connote cabbage or something.

ADÈS: Actually, they do. *In Seven Days*, the third movement, that's exactly what it's about: the creation of vegetal life, on the Third Day. Look, if you put something under the microscope you see it has millions of implications. In the opera house, those chords are used at a moment where time is completely suspended, Ariel's hypnotizing of Ferdinand . . . I thought, here we are somewhere we can't describe what's happening, Shakespeare has put a spell on us, and perhaps that's a way into some kind of pre-conscious space. Well, *In Seven Days* deals with the pre-conscious.[33]

Put another way, Adès is comfortable with material serving specifically narrative roles, or being "just chords," or functioning as some ambiguous combination of the two. A similar narrative/non-narrative feature of the score is the ascending figure which appears at moments where characters contemplate their liberation: Ariel, Miranda, and Ferdinand in the second act, joined by Caliban in the third. In a subtle move, Prospero sings an inverted form of this tendency, signaling his anxiety that all that is dear to him seems to be slipping away (Example 3.6).

Example 3.6 Liberation theme in *The Tempest*:
a) Adès, *The Tempest*, Act 2, Scene 4, R225–2 to R225.

b) Adès, "Liberation" theme in Tempest, Act 2, Scene 4, R226+7 to R226+9.

This circular, obsessive, and expansive quality of the musical material and its resonances underscore a central fact: neither Adès nor Oakes understands *The Tempest* merely as a play by Shakespeare. It is also a set of theatrical and musical conventions: burdens, catches, ventriloquism, among others. All of these interlocking musical impulses form a kind of citationality in the music that parallels that of Oakes's libretto. Adès's music is frequently referring not only to itself (as all music that develops thematically does), but also to a broader world of pre-existing musical impulses as well. In the aggregate, this material ends up constituting a grammar of musical logic, not dissimilar to the fund of textual imagery that we found throughout Oakes's libretto. Moreover, to the extent that this musical material is revisited in later works, it also reflects Adès's own observation that "artists are going to have obsessions that they return to."[34]

The centripetal and centrifugal forces in Adès's opera are arguably present in the original: Shakespeare's play is a generically liminal work in the bard's own output, wavering between public play and a court masque.[35] The opera feels most ready to spin away from its center when we recognize that Oakes's libretto is a set of utterances of fraught origin, not necessarily assigned to a particular character. This shattered quality of the text is only underscored as ghosts of other interpretations of the play surface, most acutely in how Auden's *The Sea and the Mirror* lurks in the closing measures. Yet there is a countervailing force holding the work together, at least for Adès, insofar as the opera remains a steadfastly musical enterprise. It may take place on a stage, and involve an intelligible unfolding of action, but it obeys Adès's ineffable musical logic first and foremost. We might be able to perceive the evidence of that logic by considering recurring material in the opera, or by noting certain fetish notes. Nevertheless, Adès's notion of logic appeals to a certain degree of listener intuition. Specifically, logical music in Adès's world is music that is instantly grasped as if it is in one's one mind (to return to the image we began this essay with), rather than a form of musical "argument" that must be rationally parsed.

Conclusion: The "Third Shape" and Adès's Historical Moment

The "new object" that Adès sought for *The Tempest* remains stubbornly nebulous in its contour, often easier to articulate in terms of what it isn't rather than what it is. Adès himself appreciated this dilemma when he noted that "there is a mysterious thing that happens when you set actions to music: a third shape that emerges when something non-visual like a musical score is acted out by people moving on a stage."[36] While acknowledging the "absurdity" of opera as an art form, Adès also found that this "third shape," combined with the fundamental ineffability of its musical origin, creates a necessary imperative for the way that an opera is conceived: "In opera, . . . you have this . . . absurdity of the supposed psychology of the characters on stage. I really want to do something where their psychology is not the important point. Because you can't just believe that these characters have a psychology of their own unless it is genuinely, unequivocally encoded in the music."[37] In this respect, Adès's *Tempest* holds our attention not only because of its transformative view of Shakespeare, but also for its bold demonstration of this uncompromising approach to the creation of an opera—especially the idea that the characters' interior lives (what Adès calls their "psychology") is meaningless unless it emanates clearly from the score.

In addition to providing a path through *The Tempest*, Adès's notion of a "new object" also helps to further qualify one of the longer running threads in his public image, namely as the successor to Benjamin Britten in the world of British composition. This book would not be complete without at least some consideration of Britten in Adès's reception; the casual mention of a historical lineage between Britten and Adès has appeared for most of Adès's career, in hundreds of newspaper articles about him.[38] Yet Adès himself is at best ambivalent about the comparison. During a public conversation at the Gulbenkian Foundation in 2012, one audience member asked him the question directly:

AUDIENCE MEMBER: You've quoted a lot of composers who have had an influence on your music. I wanted to ask you what you think about Britten's music.

ADÈS: Oh, well Britten, I of course knew it from a very young age. I actually particularly love a lot of the instrumental music. I like the violin concerto, I think it is simply wonderful. *A Ceremony of Carols*, and the *Missa Brevis*. I was never that attracted to the operas simply because—well, I *was* I must be honest. I did used to listen to them a lot and found them completely fascinating. But I think it got slightly spoiled for me afterwards, by the discovery of Berg and Janáček and other things. I simply found it hard to go back—not because of quality, but because somehow the English words started to put me off. I don't know what it was, it was just strange. But I'm sure I will go back to them.[39]

Adès's diplomatic response—a masterpiece of non-commitment, really—nevertheless highlights his reservation about Britten's choices for texts. In the context of Adès's philosophy of a "new object," the reasons for this reticence are clear: Britten's selection of textually rich libretti (*A Midsummer Night's Dream* being only the most evident example) worked at cross purposes with the compositional latitude necessary for the musical material to carry what Adès called the "psychology" of the characters on stage, and therefore the dramaturgy overall. Adès also criticized Britten for using compositional approaches in which the material is too easy to apprehend, for example in his critique of *Turn of the Screw* that we first encountered in this volume's previous essay on serialism. In Adès's formulation, the essence of the "third shape" of opera is that it is necessarily difficult to discern; for a composer to water down an opera's mysterious alchemy is to compromise artistically. Nor should we necessarily allow Adès to determine our experience of Britten totally: the older composer's success on the operatic stage is in no small part thanks to his brilliance in capturing his character's interior lives, whether through short scale harmonic gambits (such as the tritone-separated duet of Orford and Grimes—one of the tactics we encountered above in Adès's *Tempest*) or through the larger structures of a work like *Death in Venice*. Hence Adès's critique of Britten's opera must be read not as an absolute pronouncement about Britten's music, but rather as a reflection of Adès's embrace of ambiguity or artistic concealment, or what he called Berg's "overgrown" formal processes, whether he describes them as "fetish notes," "knight's moves," or by some other name. These fundamentally inscrutable choices in his compositional approach have been a feature of his music since the early 1990s. In the context that I have pursued here, it is also an important differentiator between his own aesthetic outlook and Britten's—the older composer having been quite vocal about preferring music that was accessible and readily interpreted by the community for which it was originally intended.[40]

If anything, *The Tempest* helps to underscore the terms on which we might see the philosophies of Britten and Adès part ways. In the face of these differences, it may be tempting to fall back on a biographical justification for a Britten–Adès lineage: they are both highly successful gay British composers who have written Shakespeare operas, have presided over the Aldeburgh festival for a time, and are noted performers and conductors as well as major composers. I would argue that Adès's degree of commitment to the priorities revealed in *The Tempest* that are in direct conflict with Britten's seem, on balance, to loom far more consequentially than any parallels of their actual lived experiences.

In a 2012 interview with Adès for the *Wall Street Journal*, interviewer Barbara Jepson noted that comparing Adès to Britten was "an appellation that causes the composer to clutch his temples in dismay." Adès then told Jepson, "Extraordinary figures like Britten only come once. I have my hands full trying to become Thomas Adès."[41] That process of self-discovery is especially on view in *The Tempest*. As celebrated as Adès's opera has been, it has not been fully understood for the aesthetic priorities it reveals in its composer's broader output. The thematic processes that are so characteristic of *The Tempest*—its "layers of desire," "tendencies," and "fetish notes"—provide a way of understanding Adès's work as a "new object" that, in a subtle but unmistakable way, pushes at the very boundaries of what an opera can and should do. As I seek to demonstrate in my next essay, this is part of a larger effort that lurks in the background of Adès's music: a desire to pull down the walls between the several arts and create synthesized aesthetic experiences that engage multiple senses simultaneously.

4

The Dilemmas of Musical Surrealism

The idea of surrealism has been one of the most consistently recurring themes in public and, to a lesser extent, scholarly discussions of Adès's significance.[1] Adès stands virtually alone as a major composer, living or dead, whose music has occasioned ongoing commentary regarding its perceived surrealistic qualities.[2] Commentators who recruit the paradigm in search of a vocabulary for discussing Adès's music have been known to arrive at a descriptive language that seems as rich in allusion and euphemism as Adès's music itself. In particular, surrealist frameworks have provided a way for critics to consider various layers of "queerness" in Adès's music (including but not limited to gender and sexuality) while avoiding a rhetoric which uses alterity and identity politics as its primary argumentative fulcra.[3] Such metaphorical approaches to writing make sense given Adès's body of work: he possesses remarkable skill at composing music which conveys several simultaneous layers of musical meaning, which has allowed him to construct sonic worlds in which multiple subjectivities might be seen to loom but are seldom directly asserted.[4]

Behind all of these issues lies the fact that surrealism is emphatically not "new." In other words, we are currently in a situation where a composer who commands considerable popular and scholarly respect is largely understood in terms of debates shaped by events that occurred between forty and one hundred years ago. Such circumstances are not problematic in absolute terms: consider the long shadow cast by Beethoven over the nineteenth century.[5] That Adès's music is framed through such wide-angle lenses following the twentieth century's radically accelerated technical innovations—during which "new" and "significant" were used virtually interchangeably for so many historiographical purposes—is only the first indication of how his case might help us to come to terms with the changing dynamics of life in the concert hall over the past twenty years.[6] Put another way, the case of Adès and surrealism asks us to reevaluate "newness" as a critical frame in the present moment.

For Adès himself, the allure of surrealism as a concept does not necessarily rest solely in its ability to convey multiple meanings at the same time or in its connection with the musical past, but rather in its apparent rhetorical capacity

Thomas Adès in Five Essays. Drew Massey, Oxford University Press (2021). © Oxford University Press.
DOI:10.1093/oso/9780199374960.001.0001.

to dodge questions of signification altogether. In an interview with Vivien Schweitzer from 2008, he allowed that surrealism is "the only 'ism' that I at all feel comfortable with."[7] But the reasons he provided for this attitude suggest that he is attracted to surrealism precisely because of its conceptual nebulousness: "Writing and playing music at all is completely surreal. You are sort of sculpting in air, which gives you complete freedom to do what you want."[8] The way in which Adès characterizes surrealism here points to one central aspect of his own aesthetic worldview: music's consistently elusive methods of signification. In an interview with Peter Culshaw, Adès suggested a more general unwillingness to specify the actual qualities of a musical experience: "When people start talking about atonal or tonal or postmodern, or whatever—I'm not being weird, but I really don't know what they are talking about."[9] In place of labels, Adès's book *Full of Noises* often asks us to observe the stunning *presence* of great music as its signal characteristic. As I will argue in this essay, listening for surrealism in Adès's music is a way for us to cast the experience of listening in a new light, or, as he put it in *Full of Noises*, "to make the real world real again."[10]

Adès is not alone in recognizing surrealism's apparent inscrutability when it comes to music. As we shall see, more than one writer has noted that surrealism proves to be a surprisingly sheer surface on which to stake a critical discourse, far more resistant to musical analogy than other movements from early twentieth-century modernism, such as expressionism and neoclassicism, which might prove relevant for situating Adès's music within a historical context. But this may ultimately be the point: the tension between the apparent specificity of surrealist aesthetics and their ultimate ambiguity in music is both the cause and effect of some of the most defining and characteristic moments in Adès's reception and his music. Moreover, as I will discuss at the end of this essay, Adès's surrealism and its limits also place him squarely within larger contemporary debates of a global art world that is struggling to find a more tractable critical vocabulary than the ones offered by the umbrella of postmodernism in its multiple manifestations.[11]

How Adès Became Surrealist

Despite the role of surrealism in many different artistic media and despite the fact that the very term "surrealism" was coined in reference to a ballet (in Apollinaire's program note to Satie and Cocteau's *Parade*), surrealists historically did not engage with music as an equal to the other arts. This lack of interest has been partially attributed to the attitudes of André Breton, the movement's fountainhead.[12] Non-programmatic instrumental music, with its perceived autonomy from the phenomenal world, has proven particularly resistant to recruitment into the surrealist habitus.[13] As a result, accounts of surrealism in music have tended to limit themselves to considerations of musical works with text, usually becoming rather unsatisfying tallies of the degree to which the music underscores the more readily perceivable surrealist quality of the text (or in the case of opera, plot).[14] Alternately, some scholars have placed an emphasis on the significance of automatism—action without conscious intervention—within the movement, which has tended to lead to the conclusion that only musical improvisation is "true" musical surrealism.[15]

Yet some of the stated objectives of Breton, at least, seem to suggest that music might be an ideal avenue for exploring elements of the surrealist project in more than just a few limited ways.[16] Surrealism promised its practitioners a direct expression of interior life, unadulterated by conventions of verisimilitude to everyday experience. In Breton's formulation, surrealism was "psychic automatism in its pure state, by which one proposes to express . . . the actual functioning of thought. Dictated by the thought, in the absence of any control exercised by reason, exempt from any aesthetic or moral concern."[17] This description, from Breton's *Surrealist Manifesto*, is not only in keeping with Breton's disdain for the novel as a genre that is too "realistic." It also points to the fundamentally intersubjective quality of Breton's vision for surrealism; if one "proposes to express" anything it must be directed at an audience, real or imagined. Although inwardly focused, in this formulation surrealism leans more toward a rhetorical mode than a meditative practice. Surrealism is social.

Adès, too, has suggested that music has at least the potential to reflect Breton's "pure functioning of thought" when he commented in *Full of Noises*, "My work is the only way I can try to understand what it might be like to be in someone else's head. When I'm writing music, I'm partly asking, 'Is it like this for you?'"[18] Breton's notion that surrealism stood apart from reason, aesthetics, and morals might also be compared to Adès's view of music as an art whose humanity lies precisely in its lack of reference to everyday life. In *Full of Noises*, Adès used the notion of absurdity—a recurring effect of so much surrealist artwork—as a rationale for the fundamental significance of music, especially opera:

> Most of the time I sit there and watch operas and think: this is all absurd. Really we shouldn't all be here! . . . [But] that is the point, the more absurd, the more indefensible, the more it makes sense . . . Operas should instead be absurd in a way that is truer than reality. But that's just the most absurd form of something that is absurd

from the start: music. Music should have no excuse, other than itself. Music is its own excuse.[19]

Although Adès doesn't make it explicit, we can sense here an affinity with the self-justifying dimension of Breton's thought, and the emphasis from both men on creating artwork that is not mediated through or stifled by rationality.

In the hands of Breton and his circle, the moral and aesthetic vacuum in which surrealism lived was nevertheless avowedly political. Breton, Aragon, Artaud, Eluard, and others made no secret of where their political sympathies lay, arraying themselves in their writings along a spectrum from anarchism to communism to a more general anti-imperialism and anti-colonialism.[20] For his part, Adès seems to have little use for this aspect of the movement. Adès has carefully cultivated his own stance of disengagement with larger questions of ethical meaning. Some of his most definitive statements on this front were made in an interview with Ian Bostridge in June of 2011:

ADÈS: I just think it matters utterly whether you choose one note or another, but it's not moral or political. It's simply to reach the truth of the idea as fully as possible.

BOSTRIDGE: All art is political, isn't it?

ADÈS: I am absolutely incapable of understanding that idea! I really don't know what that means . . . I don't think politics is going to write your piece for you. What could be more political than Beethoven's Ninth Symphony? . . . The politics of saying everybody's equal is so banal—though it wasn't banal then—but when it is put with that force, it becomes the most enormous truth. It's far beneath or above politics. Politics just seems to become irrelevant when something's put that powerfully.[21]

It has been a consistent goal of Adès to create a space for his music—for all music—which is fully autonomous, independent of the concerns of the world from whence it springs. In this sense, Adès's surrealism might be more accurately aligned with the eerily still worlds of Magritte or de Chirico rather than the more politically engaged forms of surrealism emanating from Breton's innermost circle, or even Dalí's wildly vacillating politics.[22] Nevertheless, even though Adès does not tend to reach for the extremes of the various dimensions of the surrealists' aesthetic universe—either by developing an "automatic" writing style, or seeking to foment a revolution—much of his music can be (and has been) aligned with the sightlines surveyed by the surrealists in the second quarter of the twentieth century. But how?

Given the frequent use of "surrealism" as a descriptor of Adès's sound, and given that a number of Adès's earlier works are now described as "surrealist," including *Living Toys* (1993) and *Powder Her Face* (1995), it is perhaps surprising to find that Adès's work was not routinely placed in a surrealist context until the end of 1999. Even earlier that year, one critic specifically noted that the Almeida Opera's then-current revival of *Powder Her Face* used staging that "leads us to expect a surrealism *that is utterly absent in the libretto*."[23] In the fall, though, commentators became hungry for a narrative to help frame one of the major achievements of Adès's early career, his receipt of the Grawemeyer Award for composition for his orchestral work *Asyla*. Two newspaper articles which were published within a week of the Grawemeyer Award ceremony issued the opening salvos in the public discussion of Adès's surrealist affinities. The first article was a short announcement by Patrick O'Connor about Adès's Grawemeyer, which mentioned in passing that Adès was working on an opera which used a libretto by Jean Cocteau and Raymond Radiguet (presumably *Paul & Virginie*).[24] This libretto was abandoned by Satie, and abandoned by Adès, as well, since he went on to write *The Tempest* (2003) and *The Exterminating Angel* (2015).[25] Just as scholarship on musical surrealism has emphasized works with text—and specifically with plot—so, too, was Adès's musical surrealism initially understood chiefly in terms of his operatic projects.[26]

Richard Taruskin provided the first thoroughgoing consideration of Adès's surrealist affinities in an article that appeared in the *New York Times* on 5 December 1999.[27] "A Surrealist Composer Comes to the Rescue of Modernism," the headline thundered.[28] Characterizing modernism as a set of competing priorities and focusing on two of them, Taruskin explored the tension between formalism (what he called the "sad side of the story, the one the textbooks have been telling") and eclecticism (a series of "polymorphously perverse joinings and copulations").[29] Within this context, Taruskin situated Adès's music in terms we can recognize as describing the surreal: "It achieves its special atmosphere, and projects its special meanings, through improbable sonic collages and mobiles: outlandish juxtapositions of evocative sound-objects that hover, shimmering, or dreamily revolve, in a seemingly motionless sonic emulsion."[30] In Taruskin's mind, Adès's music (he mentions the Chamber Symphony, *Asyla*, and *Powder Her Face* by name) resembles the distortions of the representative visual field that characterize the paintings of Dalí, de Chirico, and Magritte.

Taruskin's essay was also one of the first to lay out explicitly the biographical rationale for viewing Adès as a "surrealist" composer—that his mother Dawn Ades is an art historian who has specialized in surrealism. "I swear that this study in bottomless sinking and lassitude had already reminded me of Dalí's 'Persistence of Memory' (yes, the wilting watches and recognizable if unidentifiable carcass) before I put two and two together and verified the agreeable surmise that the composer's mother was in fact Dawn Ades, the author of important books on Dalí, Duchamp and the Dada and Surrealist movements." Moving from biographical skepticism to certainty in three sentences, Taruskin writes:

> What to make of this all-too-suggestive family connection is anybody's guess. But it does invite one to imagine that growing up surrounded by the captivating if academically disreputable imagery of dream realism during abstract expressionism's waning days might have given a gifted young composer the confidence to resist what was still a powerful and entirely comparable conformist pressure during his tutelary years. Mr. Adès was thus able to buck sterile utopia while avoiding the opposing pitfall of ironic pastiche.[31]

If we were to continue to ask about the possibilities of the influence of Adès's immediate milieu on his ostensible surrealism, other suggestive links beyond his mother's academic specialization materialize. His brother, Robert Ades, is a psychotherapist who has given papers on the epistemological origins of Freudian psychotherapy, and Freud's theories about the mind in turn formed part of the intellectual edifice of surrealism in the first place. His father, the translator and poet Timothy Ades, has named the surrealist poet Robert Desnos "the most exciting French poet of the last century."[32]

By the time Adès's The Tempest was first performed in 2004—a mere five years after Taruskin's article—his "surrealism" seemed practically taken for granted. Anthony Holden fell back on Dalí to describe the staging for The Tempest.[33] In his review, Mark Swed wasn't sure where Adès stood as a composer—"Did he really have a musical identity, and, if so, was he a restless romantic, modernist, surrealist, postmodernist or what?"—but did allow that Prospero's character was a distorted archetype: "Adès's pompous chorales, underpinned by tubby brass and double basses, make him a caricature of Wagner's Wotan."[34] Ivan Hewett, writing in the Telegraph, suggested that surrealism is not only an explanatory device but also a way of identifying Adès's limitations: "The comparison with Dalí is more revealing than Taruskin intended, as it points to a facile cleverness and an emotional chilliness that for me can sometimes be the aftertaste of Adès's undeniable brilliance and magic."[35] In a scholarly article, Christopher Fox noted that Adès's "scores regularly transpose elements of the surreal into music," again comparing Adès to Dalí and Magritte: "The compelling strangeness of whose works depends for its success on the evenness of painted texture and the preservation of the integrity of the picture plane and marriage of clear pictorial design with bizarre detail."[36] By 2004, a number of Adès's most important works had been retrospectively incorporated into an Adès-as-surrealist narrative.[37]

Surrealism has appeared as a watchword in the vocabulary of Adès and his immediate circle, as well, suggesting a symbiotic relationship between the reception of Adès's music and Adès's own language for discussing his music.[38] But Adès's use of the word, for all the weight that critics have put on it, suggests that he sees surrealism more generally. His use of the term in interviews reflects a range of possible meanings that *surrealism* has acquired in casual conversation, to the point where it can now be used to signify just about any event which is odd, unexpected, or out of the ordinary. In 2011, Adès remembered visiting Los Angeles for the first time in 1996 and being intoxicated by what he called its "surreal charms."[39] In a different vein, Adès's student Francisco Coll considers himself a surrealist, although he cleaves more closely to the idea of distorting a recognizable world. Describing his work *Piedras*, Coll commented: "When I write music I try to create impossible worlds in a very realistic way. This is a kind of surrealist concept."[40] Similarly, Gerald Barry, the Irish composer who has been described as Adès's "favorite colleague," relied on surrealism at a few points to describe his opera based on *The Importance of Being Earnest* in a joint interview with Adès, Stephen Fry, and Fiona Shaw.[41] Barry thought that Wilde's play itself anticipated the style: "It's obviously clearly incredibly funny, but also has all these dark, surreal qualities. The mysteriousness of it is why it is the only one of its kind."[42] Barry's use of the word here and elsewhere in the same interview suggests that he and Adès sometimes deploy surrealism as a stand-in for ideas of the uncanny and general weirdness.[43] Hence, to avoid being merely trivial, any effort to situate Adès's music within a surrealist discourse faces significant challenges of meaning.

Hearing (and Seeing) Adès's Surrealism

Before beginning a consideration of how surrealism might be seen to manifest itself in Adès's music, it is worth reiterating the fundamentally intersubjective quality of musical surrealism. Put another way, it is in general far easier to agree on when and how a poem or a painting is functioning surrealistically than it is with a piece of music. While a viewer could easily see that a melting clock in Dalí's *Persistence of Memory* is "wrong," most audience members would have a difficult time articulating what a "normal" musical texture ought to be in the first place. In Daniel Albright's words, "surrealist music [aspires] to mean wrong; and in order to mean wrong music must mean something."[44]

100 Thomas Adès in Five Essays

There have been a number of efforts to define a lexicon of surreal signifiers in music, ranging from free improvisation, to polytonality, to a more general notion of dissonance as potentially serving surrealist ends.[45] Here, though, I take a less definition-driven approach, seeking to align my reading of Adès's musical surrealism along a spectrum ranging from the more readily perceptible moments (which, in practice, means ones that are reinforced by a text) to the less obvious. Given the irreducible problems of music's "meaning," musical surrealism is present in "the music itself" only insofar as the listener perceives it to be, or in terms of what music theorist Robert Hatten has called its "stylistic competence."[46] Put another way, the actual surrealist qualities of Adès's music—or any music for that matter—can only be argued for, never decided upon.[47] Surrealism is situational.

The *fait divers*, or the journalistic telling of an extravagantly violent event, is a recurring form in surrealist art that is relevant for Adès's works from the 1990s. One method of writing surrealist stories involves reassembling words from a newspaper, such as in Roger Roughton's "Final Night of the Bath," which was put together from the 6 June 1936 edition of the *London Evening Standard*. In the opening sentence, Roughton manages to move from dull news to a strange cliffhanger: "Over two thousand people had taken tickets for this season's murder." A similar effect was achieved in Raymond Roussel's story "The Greenish Skin," which drew on his technique of selecting words with double meanings (or which were only one letter apart), and assembling them to create fantastical texts. "The Greenish Skin" opens:

> The greenish skin of the ripening plum [*La peau verdâtre de la prune un peu mûre*] looked as appetizing as anyone might wish. I therefore chose this fruit from amongst the various delicacies made ready on a silver platter for the señora's return.
> With the point of a knife I made an imperceptible hole in the delicate peel, and taking a phial from my pocket, poured in several drops of a quick working poison.
> "You betrayed me, Natte," I said in an expressionless voice. "Now meet your fate."[48]

The cool distance of the narrative voice in both of these stories heightens the impact of the already bizarre facts they recount. Similarly, Jeanette Baxter has discussed a visual version of the *fait divers* at the beginning of her essay on J. G. Ballard's *Running Wild*, offering René Magritte's painting *The Threatened Assassin* (Figure 4.1) as an emblem of surrealist fascination with enigmatic criminal moments. At first glance the narrative of the painting seems self-evident: a woman has been murdered, and the killer himself is about to meet

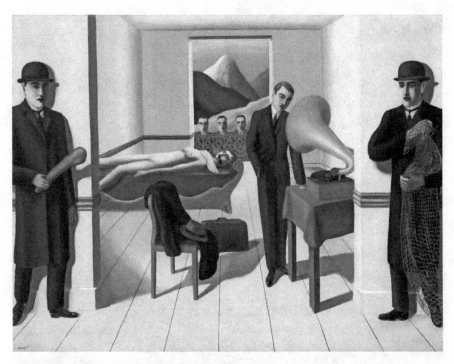

Figure 4.1 René Magritte, *L'Assassin Menacé.*

his own end. Baxter notes that questions seem to pile on top of one another as we continue to contemplate the ostensible scenario: "Who is the female victim? Why does the presumed murderer pause next to his victim in order to listen to music? Who are the three figures in the background?"[49] The gruesome murder takes on an eerie stillness as we allow the tableau to sink in. Similar depictions of crimes somehow chilled by neutral retelling can be found in Max Ernst's *Open Your Bag, My Good Man* (Figure 4.2) and in the journal *Le Surréalisme au Service de la Révolution,* which carried a section of *fait divers* recounting strange stories from the news.[50]

For Adès, one point of connection with the *fait divers* tradition is his first opera, *Powder Her Face.* This opera revisits moments in the life of the Duchess of Argyll, whose divorce case in 1963 caused a tabloid sensation in the United Kingdom. While there is no murder in *Powder Her Face,* the luridly hypersexual exploits of the Duchess form a departure from the ostensible dignity of her social rank in their own way. *Powder Her Face* is organized around a series of flashbacks while the duchess's eviction from her hotel room looms; in real life the Duchess owed some £33,000 to the Dorchester Hotel in back rent by 1990, and died in a nursing home three years later.[51] In the opera, her departure from the hotel in the final scene marks her decisive fall from society, but

Max Ernst, *Open Your Bag, My Good Man* (*illustration from La femme 100 tetes*), 1929, collage of reproductions of 19th century engravings mounted on cardboard, 6x5"   (ISBN: 0300107188)

Figure 4.2 Max Ernst, *Open Your Bag, My Good Man.*

the music performs a symbolic role above and beyond that. With the inclusion of creaking fishing reels in the score at this moment in the action, Adès also provides wordless imagery of fate finally drawing the Duchess home to death's rocky shore.

The use of fishing reels at the end is only one example of Adès's reliance on musical onomatopoeia at other pivotal moments in the opera's plot, particularly in the vocal lines. I would argue that these moments of vocal on-omatopoeia contribute in part to the surreal effect of the work overall. The dramaturgical history of opera has emphasized the idea that a theater piece which is sung would somehow engage a more elevated sphere of rhetoric than the merely spoken; disrupting the sung fabric of the opera can be used for striking effect. This is often the reason provided for why Samiel, the evil char-acter in Weber's *Der Freischütz*, speaks rather than sings, or why Puck's role is spoken in Britten's *A Midsummer Night's Dream*. So for Adès to drop down to "lowly" unsung vocalizations at several crucial moments in the action ought to engender a sensation of sous-realism rather than sur-realism. Yet some of the moments of musical onomatopoeia in *Powder Her Face* have precisely the opposite effect, because their rupture of the diegetic frame bursts forth to the audience at moments of maximum dramatic effect.[52]

The fourth scene is the most famous example of this phenomenon, as the duchess fellates a waiter in a vowel-less aria (Example 4.1). Philip Hensher, the librettist, wrote in 2008 that this scene is what gave *Powder Her Face* "a life be-yond the first run."[53] He continued:

> The notorious photographs of the Duchess of Argyll "performing" (I loved the word) fellatio on a stranger was at the centre of her divorce case. From day one, I had told Tom [Adès] that the opera had to contain "a blow-job aria—you know, it begins with words and ends with humming." When he had recovered, he agreed, though a little nervously.[54]

This scene has sat at the center of the opera ever since, both for its advocates and its glossators ("This opera blows," D. L. Groover dourly punned in a nega-tive review of a 2011 production in Houston).[55] At least two productions have used this scene's departure from the "normal" narrative style of the opera (i.e., sung drama) as an occasion for the staging to take on surreal elements, as well. In the 2008 production from the Royal Opera House, a single supernumerary nude emerges from a bed (which, itself, is surreally shaped like a makeup compact), standing above the character of the Waiter, played in this produc-tion by Iain Paton (Figure 4.3).[56] This strategy was taken to an extreme in the New York City Opera's production in 2013, when some two dozen nude men circulated on stage during the scene (Figure 4.4). The director Jay Scheib and his creative team explained in the program that the waiter is but one instance of the Duchess's liaisons, describing the supernumeraries as "memories of many, many affairs" who "crowd the room."[57] Yet neither the Duchess nor the Waiter ever acknowledge the supernumeraries during this scene in the production. If they are "memories," Scheib's production invites the interpretation that they

Example 4.1 Adès, *Powder Her Face*, Scene 4, mm. 262–70.

are somehow repressed, submerged beneath the plane of the Duchess's conscious thought. Such an approach is only the first example we will see of the
subconscious, or even more generally the mind's inner dialogue, providing
the animating cognitive dissonance for a surrealist experience.

Joan Rodgers in POWDER HER FACE
Royal Opera House, 2008

Figure 4.3 Still from Royal Opera House Production of *Powder Her Face*, 2008.

This scene's sensationalism has become something of a shorthand for the so-called antics of the entire opera. But the particular musical technique of onomatopoeia is anticipated in the second scene of the opera by the pervasive laughing notated throughout. In this scene, the Lounge Lizard, the Duchess, and the Confidante are waiting for the arrival of the Duke, and the ennui is palpable. Musically, the existential boredom of the three characters progresses through the scene as the Lounge Lizard and the Confidante gossip about the Duchess's first divorce, and ultimately the Lounge Lizard offers a "pantomime" to the Duchess, performing along to a recording of a song that apparently has been written about her.[58] Yet the running-down-the-clock quality of the scene is perhaps musically best represented by the trio's progressively more joyless laughter in the first half of the scene (Example 4.2), which lurches to a halt as the characters seem to become aware that they themselves are the cause of their own boredom.

Similarly, the staging and music in the sixth scene work together to give this vocal onomatopoetic strategy its apotheosis. In this scene, the Judge reads his verdict at the divorce trial, with exaggerated bellowing in octaves opening the scene (Example 4.3). In the film of the opera the staging becomes gradually

Powder Her Face, Photo © Pavel_Antonov, Allison Cook

Figure 4.4 Still from New York City Opera Production of *Powder Her Face*, 2013.

more perverse: the Judge is shown wearing fishnet stockings and red high heels, and then reappears in the Duchess's hotel room, slashing at his chest with a tube of lipstick and staging a mock crucifixion of himself above the Duchess's fireplace as he ends his aria (Figure 4.5).[59] The lofty musical plane of the opera is momentarily shattered at this moment as the Judge abandons song altogether and, following a passage of stuttering, finally splutters: "I cannot express my horror at what I have discovered" (Example 4.4). These passages in *Powder Her Face* pursue their surreal signification not by attempting to reveal a plane of experience which floats above the normative one of the opera, but by stomping on the conceit of opera itself. It is the musical equivalent of the opening scene in Luis Buñuel's film *Un Chien Andalou* where a woman's eye is held as if to be sliced open. The film then cuts to show a thin trail of cloud passing in front of the moon. Just as we think the moment of violence will be depicted in this symbolic way, the metaphor is trampled as the film cuts back to show the woman's eye being gruesomely slit open on screen, leaving nothing to the imagination.

The expressive potential of the non-sung, or semi-sung, vocal writing in *Powder Her Face* does more than merely momentarily rupture the diegetic

Example 4.2 Adès, *Powder Her Face*, Scene 2, mm. 87–98.

2

Figure 4.5 Still from film production of *Powder Her Face* (Kultur International Films, Ltd.: DC 10002, 1999).

frame of the opera. In Hensher's discussion of the origins of the fellatio scene, he explained some of his conceptual influences:

> I had been reading, I think, Wayne Koestenbaum's books on opera, all very keen on the idea that opera is both a way of giving women a voice and a sexual statement, but only as a means of ultimately silencing them. The image of a woman being brutally silenced through sex was, I thought, a powerful one, and the Duchess, in the opera, is specified as being silenced twice: first by sex and then by death. That second silencing, with a microphone being dragged round a gong and fishing reels being wound in the orchestra, turned out to be the easier one for music critics to admire.[60]

Hensher's précis of Koestenbaum's book *The Queen's Throat: Opera, Homosexuality, and the Mystery of Desire* is true up to a point insofar as Koestenbaum does consider at length female roles in opera. But *The Queen's Throat* is perhaps more accurately described as a memoiristic exploration of the history of gay men as devotees of opera, and the role of silence looms throughout the book less as a symbol of misogyny than as one of gay repression. Writing about the experience of watching one of his friends lip-synch to

Example 4.3 Adès, *Powder Her Face*, Scene 6, mm. 118–41.

Example 4.3 *Continued*

2

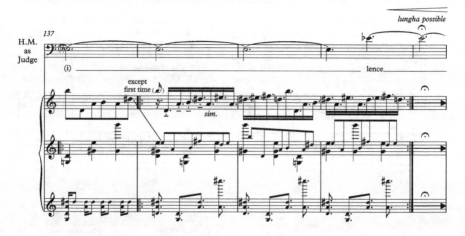

Example 4.4 Adès, *Powder Her Face,* Scene 6, mm. 294–302.

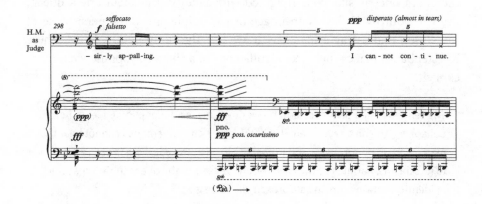

Example 4.4 *Continued*

a Maria Callas recording, Koestenbaum writes: "In the era of Silence = Death, the opera queen's silence is freighted with fatality. The silent opera queen, drowned out by Callas, is an image of gay helplessness, the persistence of the closet, and a tragic inability to awaken the body politic."[61] Elsewhere Koestenbaum makes the queer significance of a silenced soprano even more explicit:

> The tendency of a diva's voice to break down makes queer people feel at home. Collapsing, the diva says, "I am discontinuous. I am vulnerable. I cannot bear the martyrdom of performance and exposure." In crisis the vocal organ calls attention to its schisms, narrates its own history, and reveals to the queer subject that voice or identity is always torn in half, broken, dispossessed.[62]

By citing Koestenbaum, Hensher is ultimately dropping a hairpin, offering the means to a gay reading of this scene without naming it, and in doing so pointing to another dimension of the fellatio scene, namely to its potential to serve as a site of identification for queer audiences. The collision of the queer with the surreal in the fellatio scene is but one example of how surrealism can provide a proxy discourse for the not-quite-said.[63] Hensher and Adès are both openly gay, yet have avoided conspicuous markers of difference or explorations of intensely homoerotic subject matter (at least by the standards of a writer like Wayne Koestenbaum). Adès has noted that he has "thought about doing an opera with two male leads, but that would be too gay, too contrived."[64] As we shall see, this is not the only moment where Adès chooses to stay in the shadowlands of the not-quite-said, thereby retaining the expressive power of the distortion of the notional frame that is so central to surrealist effects. Yet Adès has composed a work with two male protagonists, although it is not an opera.

Adès's song *Life Story* deals in the hazy intersection of homosexuality and surrealism in ways that are at least as laden with signification as *Powder Her Face*. The grim inevitability of *Life Story*—which sets Tennessee Williams's poem about a sexual encounter in a seedy hotel room immediately before two men burn to death in one another's arms—approaches its surrealism (and recapitulates the *fait divers* genre) in a somewhat different way. The cover of the sheet music for the piece (designed by a third party but presumably in consultation with Adès) already suggests a visual allusion to the language of Magritte's *La Reproduction Interdite* (Figures 4.6 and 4.7). It reproduces a photo by Gilberte Brassaï, *Mirrored Wardrobe in a Brothel*, with a slightly off-kilter portrait of two figures, one clothed, one nude, facing a mirror, both with their backs to the frame. A close look reveals the nude figure to be female (the faint outline of a necklace and high heels can be discerned), but Brassaï's photo is remarkable for its chilling anonymity, in part because of the faceless androgyny of both the nude and, to a lesser extent, the clothed man in his blousy shirt. This cover begs the question of what will be shown and what will be hidden on the pages its glossy cardstock contains.

Williams's text is discreet yet unmistakable in identifying the encounter as specifically between two men. Narrated predominantly in the second person (the poem begins: "After you've been to bed together for the first time"), Williams relies on genderless pronouns and subject phrases throughout ("the other party"; "they say"; "one of you falls asleep"), lending an air of mystery to the situation upon a first gloss of the poem. Only twice, when the bodies of the characters are referenced, does Williams specify a gender ("one of you rises to pee / and gaze at himself with mild astonishment in the bathroom mirror"; "the other one does likewise with a lighted cigarette in his mouth"), and does so practically in passing. Even at these moments of gender specification, there is just enough ambiguity to provide an air of plausible deniability to the gay subtext of the poem, and, therefore, the encounter that it narrates. As Philip Brett and many others have explored at length elsewhere, the politics of labeling—and of resisting labels to—same-sex relationships

Figure 4.6 Magritte, *La Reproduction Interdite*.

has been a battleground of the cultural politics of homosexuality in the twentieth century, and Williams's poem, published in 1956, is an artifact of that phenomenon.[65]

For its part, Adès's musical setting of *Life Story* develops this brooding unease of post-coital anonymity that Williams's poem evokes. The opening piano gesture (Example 4.5) is inherently ambiguous, refusing in its low register to allow any decisive tonal center to establish itself, with trills clouding the part as it develops. This lurching passagework in the piano grates uncomfortably against the long lyrical melodies of the soprano, which slink and slide chromatically through the vocal line. The structural centers of the work are

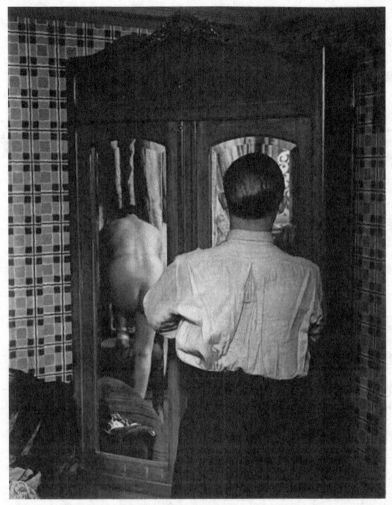

Figure 4.7 Gilberte Brassaï, *Mirrored Wardrobe in a Brothel* (used in cover for Adès, *Life Story*, London, UK: Faber Music Ltd., 1997).

two extended melismas on "oh," together consuming twelve of the seventy-nine measures of the song (Example 4.6). On their own, the melismas perform a narrative trick, since on the one hand they are the only lines in the poem that directly quote a character's speech ("And they say oh, oh, oh, oh, oh" / "And you're saying oh, oh, oh, oh, oh") but on the other hand they are extended to such length that they become pure vocalization, two existential howls puncturing the otherwise matter-of-fact vocal part. Both melismas, like the laughter in the aforementioned second scene of *Powder Her Face*, lurch awkwardly to a halt. In this sense we might hear these melismas as "surreal"

Example 4.5 Adès, *Life Story*, mm. 1–5. © 1997 Faber Music Ltd, reproduced by kind permission of the publishers.

Example 4.6 Adès, *Life Story*, mm. 36–40; mm. 61–69.

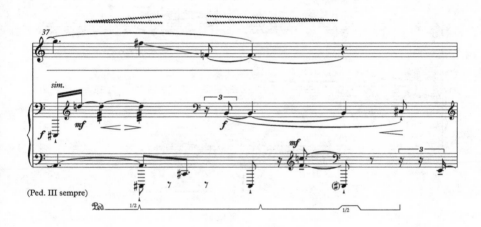

Example 4.6 *Continued*

Example 4.6 *Continued*

Example 4.6 *Continued*

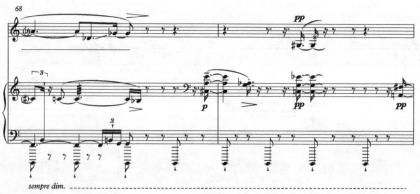

moments in the texture of the song overall, since they lift us out of the frank narrative style of the rest of the setting. Adès further invites distortion of the pure melisma by instructing the singer that "the late style of Billie Holiday is recommended as a model" throughout and to "modify vowel when and where required" during the melismas. The melismas are also undergirded by a peculiar pedal point, the first on C-sharp and the second on B. In both cases the damper of the second lowest instance of the pitch is held down with the sostenuto pedal, while the lowest instance is forcefully struck at roughly even intervals, creating a ringing and thunderous accompaniment to the vocal line which is unlike anything else in the work, and reinforcing the sense that these melismas are somehow separate from the prevailing diegetic frame of the rest of the song.[66] *Life Story* ends with a practically whispered final line of Williams's poem, which recasts the entire meaning of the work in retrospect (Example 4.7). In this way, Adès breaks down the sung vocal line in a manner not dissimilar from his handling of key moments in *Powder Her Face*.

Taken together, these moments from *Life Story* and *Powder Her Face* raise the larger question of the interpenetration of surrealism with not only the idea of queerness but also with the notion of the uncanny in music. Conceptually, surrealism and the uncanny are at least partially coextensive, insofar as both ideas claim automata, the eerie, and the abnormal within their purview.[67] The notion of a "double" plays a central role in both. Historically, the first discussion of the uncanny in the arts was roughly contemporaneous with the advent of surrealism, receiving its signal exposition in Freud's eponymous essay published in 1919.[68] As Richard Cohn put it, a "central component" of uncanniness for Freud was "the tendency of the repressed familiar to emanate in a strangely defamiliarized form."[69] E. T. A. Hoffmann's story "The Sandman" performs important work in Freud's argument, the recurring malevolent character of Coppela / Coppelius / the Sandman being one of the key elements of the story's uncanny effect. From there, Freud extrapolates the idea of an ominous doppelgänger as one harbinger of the uncanny. The doubles of the preceding examples from Adès's music—the paired melismas of *Life Story*; the doubled nude bodies in the staging of the fellatio scene in *Powder Her Face*— fit snugly with the notion of doubling as a harbinger of the uncanny.

Perhaps the most powerful instance of doubling in *Powder Her Face* can be located in the simple fact that only four singers perform all of the roles in the opera, so that the Lounge Lizard in Scene 2 is performed by the tenor, who reappears as the Waiter in Scene 4, and the same bodies are constantly presented anew over the course of the opera. On the one hand this is a practical expedient for staging an opera with a limited cast; on the other hand we have characters strangely embodying one another such that it is not always

Example 4.7 Adès, *Life Story*, mm. 77–79.

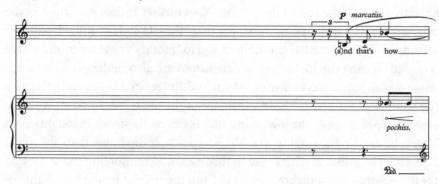

clear how they do or do not relate. Consider the disorientation, for example, of watching the Duke, as Judge, read the verdict at his own divorce trial. Similarly, the Waiter's sneering humiliation of the Duchess at the end of the fourth scene is placed in relief as we recall the same singer performing the sycophantic pantomime from the second scene.[70] We can only see the Judge as a new character if we willfully forget—that is, repress—the memory of having seen the very same performer only one scene prior, as Duke, carrying out his own extramarital liaison.

Adès's most recent opera, *The Exterminating Angel*, draws on striking repeated sections to achieve part of its surrealist effect. Some of these repetitions are present in the original film by Luis Buñuel. In Buñuel's film, the characters must restage exactly the piano performance of Blanca in order to finally escape the room that they are trapped in; they also apparently arrive at the dinner party twice, without further explanation. Finally, the end of the film mirrors the beginning with its implication that all of the villagers now, rather than merely the guests, are about to become trapped within the church. Adès adds to this fabric of uncanny resemblances by adding structural parallels in each act of the opera. Blanca's piano playing in the first and third act is also eerily reflected in the middle act by the "Over the sea" aria. The two lovers, Beatriz and Eduardo, punctuate the action of each act with duets—expressing first love, then desperation, then death—which stand apart from the rest of the action.

Lloyd Whitesell has explored how strange characters, and strangely repeating characters, can engender uncanny moments in opera which, in his words, also "reinforce the implication of an emboldened queer presence."[71] Whitesell focuses on the operas of Britten, providing examples of this phenomenon from *The Turn of The Screw* and *Death in Venice* and hence making explicit the interplay between uncanniness and queer readings. Put another way, the surreal, the uncanny, and the queer can overlap in ways that mutually reinforce one another, and while they can ostensibly be pried apart, they function as a chord in moments like the fellatio scene, adding up to more than the sum of their individual parts. Other scholars have emphasized two other aspects of Freud's ideas about the uncanny—a persistent uncertainty as to whether an object is alive or dead, and the uncanny's (*unheimlich* in Freud's original German) conceptual rapport with the notion of "home" (*heimlich*)—which I will explore in due course.[72]

Uncanny or not, Adès's engagement with surrealism goes beyond the depiction of queer moments in opera and song. We might also locate surrealism in Adès's vocal music through more elusive manipulations of stylistic conventions.[73] In these contexts the "not-quite-said" element of musical surrealism sheds the (homo-)erotic tinge of *Powder Her Face* and *Life Story* and becomes a more abstract process of detecting and interpreting musical signifiers. Of course, such an approach requires us to acknowledge the escalating problem of apprehending musical meaning as we move away from the comfortable terrain of text-music relationships.[74] In a reply to a letter to the editor about his *New York Times* article, Taruskin responds to this issue by pointing out that music need not necessarily have a textual or programmatic reference point in order to achieve a "surreal" quality. "Surrealism achieves many of its effects by juxtaposing items of ordinary experience in extraordinary ways," Taruskin writes, offering the example of polytonality in the hands of Darius Milhaud as one example of a way this can be achieved in an instrumental texture.[75] Mere juxtaposition, however, is obviously not a meaningful criterion in isolation, since Adès is hardly the only composer to use distorted conventions for expressive ends. Many early twentieth-century composers—including Mahler, Ives, Debussy, Stravinsky, and Schoenberg, to name only a handful—reimagined existing genres and norms in novel ways.[76] In the 1980s the Polish composers Stanisław Krupowicz and Paweł Szymański coined the term "surconventionalism" to describe their approach and in so doing offered a further refinement of ways in which musical genres can function surreally. Szymański described his Sonata (1982) as being composed of "a set of elements belonging to a certain convention, governed by rules which have nothing to do with this convention, [like] elements of reality which appear in surrealistic paintings as an extraneous order to this reality." For his part, Krupowicz describes convention as "what is known, what the listener registers as known," and posits that surconventionalism, therefore, is "an art of composing contexts."[77]

We might understand Adès's song *Brahms* (2001), for baritone and orchestra, as a work which "composes context" for a setting of an Alfred Brendel poem through exaggerated use of some of Brahms's own signature techniques. Edward Venn has explored this work at length, emphasizing what he called the "hauntological" elements of Adès's setting, considering how the specters of Brahms, Schoenberg, and others loom in Adès's composition.[78] The song sets a poem from Brendel's volume *One Finger Too Many*, which describes the ghost of Brahms arriving in the dead of night, smoking, singing, and playing the piano.[79] We might expect Adès's setting to latch on to Brendel's description of Brahms playing the family piano ("Even worse though / is his piano playing / This wading through chords and double octaves / wakes even the children from their deep sleep"), but Adès instead draws on other sounds characteristic of Brahms. Most obviously, Adès's exaggerated use of descending thirds harkens back to Brahms's heavy use of thirds in his Fourth Symphony (Example 4.8a and b).[80] Similarly, Adès's melodic line relies on a careful development and liquidation of thematic material, as Brahms often did at climatic points in his music (Example 4.9a and b). One can certainly speculate as to whether Adès relied on these as specific signifiers for Brahms—both

Example 4.8

a) Adès, *Brahms*, mm. 1–13. © 2009 Faber Music Ltd, reproduced by kind permission of the publishers.

b) Brahms, Fourth Symphony, Finale, mm. 1–8.

Example 4.8 *Continued*

Allegro energico e passionato

Allegro energico e passionato

Example 4.9

a) Adès, *Brahms*, mm. 86–99.

Example 4.9 *Continued*

b) Brahms, Rhapsody in B minor, Op. 79, No. 1, mm. 49–63.

techniques appear in Schoenberg's landmark essay "Brahms the Progressive" as evidence of Brahms's significance for twentieth century music—in an effort to deliberately nod to a modernist conception of Brahms's compositional approach.[81] Nevertheless, these moments are decidedly "surconventional" insofar as they extend and elaborate a technique in a way that is at once identifiable and distorted. The absolute disintegration that Adès achieves by having the baritone sing the word "Brahms" twenty-five times in a row near the end (first in groups of three, then in awkward pairs of leaping sevenths and ninths, and then in a pair of descending scales) is demonstrative to the point of comedy.[82]

But what of Adès's purely instrumental work, and its possible rapport with surrealism? Writers have already noted that Adès's Piano Quintet grotesquely distorts sonata form.[83] The single, massive movement which makes up the work proudly wears its sonata form on its sleeve, replete with a full repeat of the exposition. Yet the recapitulation is ruthlessly foreshortened, leading to what Christopher Fox has called a "spectacular contraction" and Tom Service has named a "black hole."[84] Philip Stoecker has published an extensive analysis of the pitch material of the Piano Quintet, focusing on Adès's disciplined use of three-voice aligned interval cycles.[85] Fox has suggested that this economy of pitch material can, in its way, be considered surrealist. He notes that when it comes to painting,

> What is depicted may be fantastic nonsense but there is a logic within the depiction itself which is reassuringly reminiscent of codes of visual representation familiar from earlier schools of narrative painting. A similar process takes place within Adès's music: he presents us with an extraordinarily inventive wealth of melodic and harmonic detail but virtually all of it can be related to a few intervallic relationships, usually introduced at the beginning of the work.[86]

The surrealism in a work like the Piano Quintet may also be more readily perceptible than the sometimes arcane pitch processes that Stoecker explores. Fox described the "palpable shock of disbelief [that] ran through the avantgardiste audience [at the premiere] when Adès turned back 16 pages of score to begin the repeat."[87] The moment of recognition—coupled with incomprehension—that Fox reports turns the listener's expectations back on themselves in a manner similar to the previously discussed scene in Buñuel's *Un Chien Andalou* or Magritte's *La Reproduction Interdite*. By doing nothing—by merely carrying out the mundane imperative of repeating the exposition—Adès reflected back to the audience members their own insatiable thirst for the new. Adès's repeat was, by the perverse logic with which new works are so often heard in the contemporary concert hall, a surrealistically confrontational way to skew an audience's expectations.

Adès's *Mazurkas* include an alternate, more private form of musical surrealism. The second mazurka provides two staves for the right hand. "Play this," instructs the one; "hear this," instructs the other (Example 4.10). In a reductively literal sense, here Adès asks the performer to imagine a layer of music which is unheard but floats above—"*sur*"—the sounding work. In this sense, Adès's surrealist moments span the range from the public to the private, allowing the possibility for moments which do not engage the audience at all, but are rather intended for either the private pleasure of the performer even for Adès's own secret amusement.

In some of Adès's works, multiple ways of understanding or identifying the bending of convention can be simultaneously deployed. The *Sonata da Caccia* at first blush seems firmly neoclassical in its orientation. It is a two-fold

Example 4.10 Adès, Second Mazurka, mm. 1–6. © 2010 Faber Music Ltd, reproduced by kind permission of the publishers.

neoclassicism, since Adès's choice of instrumentation—Baroque oboe, horn in F, and harpsichord—is taken from Debussy, who had planned the same instrumentation for his unrealized fourth instrumental sonata. Adès writes that the *Sonata da Caccia* "could be imagined as a 'homage' to Debussy and Couperin, in the manner of the latter's *L'Apothéose de Corelli* or *L'Apothéose de Lulli*."[88] It is an homage to an homage. At the same time, the *Sonata da Caccia* can be situated along surrealist lines by considering it alongside Adès's other compositions which look to the past for their inspiration. As discussed in a previous essay in this volume, the external reference in *Darknesse Visible* is Dowland's song "In Darknesse Let Mee Dwell." Yet Dowland's original is so distorted here as to be absorbed beyond recognition in Adès's texture— the "real" seems to have been sublimated, making a "surreal" effect impossible. On the other side, Adès's *Three Studies from Couperin* seem most intelligibly understood as arrangements of Couperin's *Pieces de Clavecin*, even though they, too, depart significantly from the original in certain moments (for example at the clangorous end of the second movement, "Les Tours de Passe-Passe"). Yet in *Sonata da Caccia*, what we might consider opposing poles of absorption and distortion are held in balance, so that the work never completely surrenders to Adès's own predilections, nor ever settles into mere stylistic imitation. One emblematic moment of this is the opening of the second movement, where Adès writes a lilting tune for the horn and oboe (Example 4.11), doubled in thirds. Despite its highly syncopated look on the page it sounds relatively straightforward when heard. At the same time, this carefree tune is accompanied by a harpsichord line in the lowest reaches of the instrument, a distorted gurgling that undercuts any sense of classical balance in the texture. This passage might be more constructively described as neoclassical if only Adès had transposed the harpsichord part up an octave or two. In its actual incarnation, it serves as an example of the surrealism that a purely instrumental passage can achieve when it deliberately flouts an expectation (in this case, the range of the harpsichord). Put another way, what we hear is not the nominally neoclassical harpsichord part, but its sinister double, rumbling in the bass. It is a musical doppelgänger, which brings us back to the notion of the uncanny.

Surrealism from the Inside Out

Up to this point, my approach has been to presuppose that certain works by Adès have a surrealist dimension and then to consider how we might locate that dimension in the musical text. In Edward Venn's discussion of musical meaning in *Asyla*, he notes that this style of analysis, by no means uncommon,

Example 4.11 Adès, *Sonata da Caccia*, ii, mm. 2–11. © 2003 Faber Music Ltd, reproduced by kind permission of the publishers.

Example 4.11 *Continued*

ought to be balanced by an approach which considers the musical text and asks how it might yield other potential readings.[89] The final two examples in this essay are an effort to do just that.

In Richard Cohn's essay about musical representations of the uncanny, he exhaustively explores the signifying potential of a curious chord progression—E major to C minor (and all its transpositions)—which has been understood by numerous commentators and composers to possess a particularly "uncanny" quality. Cohn called this progression a "hexatonic pole," and provided examples of it ranging from Gesualdo (in "Moro Lasso") to Strauss (in the opening of *Salome*) and Schoenberg (at the beginning of his String Trio).[90] For Cohn, as for Freud, the uncanny is a multifaceted and opaque experience, rather than a simple signifier. Cohn emphasizes that Freud's notion of a "defamiliarized home" is central to the musically uncanny effect of this progression. Cohn also notes that the German antonym to uncanny, *heimlich*, itself denotes not just the familiar, but also the "private, secret, [and] clandestine." In this sense the *unheimlich* is not only the opposite of *heimlich*, but also, paradoxically, its extreme intensification. As Cohn puts it, we experience the uncanny when "the clandestine is transformed into something so interior, so familiar, that it is hidden from the viewing eye and inquiring mind."[91]

For Cohn, these opposing qualities exist in a series of intersecting tensions. When it comes to actual progressions of hexatonic poles in music, he notes that the chords "both are and are not triads; they both are and are not consonant. In terms of the music theoretic writings of Freud's contemporaries, their status as entities is both real and imaginary, both alive and dead."[92] This stems in part from the fact that the two chords, since they come from separate diatonic collections, cannot both be heard within the same tonal context. Cohn also points out that even in a "tonally indeterminate environment," it is impossible to decide which of the two triads is more important, since each chord contains the other's leading tone, as well as the flattened sixth scale degree above the opposing chord, leading to what Cohn called "double leading-tone reciprocity." He continues:

> Each triad of the pair powerfully "summons" the other. Their relationship constitutes an exceptionally potent instance of . . . reciprocal exchange. Each triad destabilizes the other; Lendvai writes that they tonally "neutralize" each other. Such relationships are among "the weirdest cases that arise": they are the musical equivalent of Escher's hands, which draw each other's cuffs.[93]

Such weirdness posed significant problems in the history of music theory, and, as Cohn argues, also engaged larger metaphysical issues insofar as it became impossible for theorists to determine which one of the chords in a given hexatonic pole was "real"—that is, served a bona fide tonal function—and which one was an "appearance"—that is, constituted a foreground feature incidental to the larger tonal fabric of a work.[94]

Hexatonic poles, then, have historically held significant potential for purely formal uses, but have also become laden with extramusical significance. It is fair to ask, therefore, how we might interpret their status as the building blocks of the third movement of Adès's piano concerto *In Seven Days* (2008). We have already encountered this work as one of Adès's most thoroughgoingly serialist pieces in a previous essay; it also proves relevant to this discussion. This concerto depicts the creation myth of the Book of Genesis, and its movements, all played *attacca*, are titled as follows:

  i. Chaos—Light—Dark
 ii. Separation of the waters into sea and sky
iii. Land—Grass—Trees
 iv. Stars—Sun—Moon
  v. Fugue: Creatures of the Sea and Sky
 vi. Fugue: Creatures of the Land
vii. Contemplation

In the third movement—the moment where life appears on earth—Adès rearranges the material into a serialist framework. The tone row for this movement is nothing more than an outlining of one hexatonic pole nested inside another, as a rereading of Table 2.2 will reveal.[95] In its initial statement, B major–G minor sits inside a D-flat minor (spelled C-sharp minor)–F Major progression.[96] In the movement, only the interior hexatonic pole is actually heard as a progression, since the final triad of the row elides with a transposition of the row. This means that Cohn's chord sequence is heard throughout the movement at all possible levels of transposition. In terms of the music's formal structure, Cohn's discussion of a hexatonic pole's mutually animating qualities provides another way of understanding Adès's description of the musical "spiral" that the pitch material creates. Furthermore, insofar as major and minor triads are the most familiar sonorities to our ears—the most *heimlich*, in Cohn's formulation—their presence in this serial context can be parsed as an expression of the repressed familiar sounding out from within the ostensibly disorienting context of a twelve-tone composition.[97] The *heimlich*, in a word, has sprung forth from the *unheimlich*. Finally, if we look to add one more work to what Cohn calls his "gallery of hexatonic poles," the programmatic dimension of *In Seven Days* aligns with the general shape of Cohn's other examples: the hexatonic poles appear at the precise moment where life is created, which is arguably the most fundamental possible example of the uncanny and surrealist trope of the inanimate suddenly becoming alive.

Yet this movement of *In Seven Days* resists a comfortable association with surrealism and the uncanny on both formal and hermeneutic fronts. Intramusically, the hexatonic poles are heard in a "tonally indeterminate environment," effectively "neutralizing" (to borrow Cohn's terminology) their own extraordinary tonal power. Extramusically, it is hard to forget the ghoulish and sinister trappings of the uncanny. Freud's example of "dismembered limbs . . . feet which dance by themselves" is among the most striking instances that he summons in his essay.[98] Although we can force the issue and insist that the moment of life appearing on earth—the stated program of this moment in the work—is the foundational example of supernatural animation, it is still hard to think of the Genesis creation myth as "uncanny" in the way that Freud and others have understood the term, if for no other reason than that the miraculous need not be eerie.[99] Perhaps the crux of the matter is that Freud's uncanny is fundamentally a subjective state in which there must be an *observer*.[100] Since the third movement of *In Seven Days* depicts a moment before the dawn of human subjectivity, the degree to which it can meaningfully be understood in terms of signifying something uncanny is by definition limited.

From a strictly formalist perspective, the lure of hexatonic poles musically lies in their very instability, their heightened degree of ambiguity. But what about ambiguity of signification? There is one moment in his career where Adès explicitly shied away from a moment of surreal signification, in his decision to disavow the program for *Living Toys* (1993), for precisely the reason that he seemed to see its expressive potential as constrained by too specific a meaning. In its way, therefore, this work is a fitting final example to consider

because it shows the limits of the territory in Adès's music which might be surveyed along surrealist lines. Adès wrote the following epigram for the work:

> When they asked him what he wanted to be, the boy did not name any of the men's
> occupations, as they had all hoped he would, but replied: "I am going to be a hero,
> and dance with angels and bulls, and fight with bulls and soldiers, and die a hero in
> a distant place, and be buried a hero." Hearing this child's words, the men felt small,
> understanding that they were not heroes, and that their lives were less substantial
> than the dreams which surrounded him like toys.
>
> **—from the Spanish.**[101]

Of course, the notion that dreams might be even more substantive than reality is an idea explored extensively by the surrealists, Dalí and his "hand-
painted dream photographs" being perhaps the most well-known example.[102]
Moreover, the program note which Adès has provided for live performances
of *Living Toys*—at least until he disavowed the program—further elaborates
the work's surrealist program. First, he describes the structure of the piece
in terms of a multimedia juxtaposition: "The child/hero's dream-adventures
form the five 'figurative' sections, offset by three more volatile, dynamic
paragraphs: painting versus film, perhaps."[103] In so doing, Adès proposes a
pseudomorphism between the arts which Apollinaire and Satie both recog-
nized as an important element of the original surrealist work, *Parade*.[104]

The program continues steadily through evocative surrealist moments.
In the first movement, an aurochs (an extinct forerunner to modern cattle)
rather than a bull charges into the ring to challenge the young matador.
The "painting" movements rely on anagrammatic wordplay in which the
surrealists would surely have delighted (the movements are respectively titled BALETT [*sic*], BATTLE, TABLET).[105] Later, Adès describes sharp turns
in subjectivity: the child/hero goes from experiencing a dream to starring in
a film in which he is "dismantling a great computer, whose vast intelligence
dwindles to a wilting Vicwardian music hall waltz"—referencing Stanley
Kubrick's *2001*. Despite the specificity of this wild program, Adès later dis-
tanced himself from it. "I invented this story, which is in the score, and said
it was 'from the Spanish': that was after I'd written the piece, and I felt I had
to find a way of explaining it. Wrongly, of course."[106] He goes on to explain
that "Aurochs and Angels" was a phrase from the last paragraph of Nabokov's
novel *Lolita* which appealed to him, nothing more.

The disavowed program for *Living Toys* seems to indicate one limit of surrealist signification in the music of Adès: it can never over-specify. Once the carefully delineated program is set aside (perhaps only *In Seven Days* approaches

a similar level of programmatic detail in Adès's instrumental oeuvre), we are left with a rather difficult work to parse into its narrative components. The movements of *Living Toys* are performed without pause, making the actual changes of scene described in the program somewhat obscure. It is of course possible to force ourselves to imagine that surrealism might obtain if the work were to be heard with score in hand. Certainly the trumpets, castanets, and clapping in the movement "Aurochs" are at least evocative of a vaguely "Spanish" texture. Yet once the program is removed, *Living Toys* seems to align poorly with the other intersections with surrealism in Adès's music.

Musical Surrealism and the Historical Now

Adès's decision to disavow the program for *Living Toys* points toward one of his recurring concerns, the desired sense of instability in his compositions. As he explained in *Full of Noises*: "I don't believe in stability, I don't think it exists in life . . . The moment I put a note down on paper it starts to slide around on the page."[107] This idea of music's instability permeates his comments in *Full of Noises*, and in time it becomes clear that instability is enmeshed with what Adès calls music's "fundamental indefensibility"—that it should not have or even require an ultimate rationale or purpose. One of the dangers of revising his music, he worries, is that he "can take it too far and destroy the unpredictability, the indefensibility—and lose the piece and start writing the obituary . . . To work it's got to have friction in it. Music should be inexplicable and indefensible."[108] Similarly, trying to hear surrealism throughout Adès's music runs the risk of "writing an obituary" for its reception. Others have also noted that overarticulating a particular aesthetic for a composer's work can tend to deaden it. "The nice thing about an ism," Taruskin sharply observed in a different context, "is how quickly it becomes a wasm."[109] Venn, too, is cautious about trying to describe the broad frame of Adès in terms of a single conceptual frame: "such categorisations, whether modernist, postmodernist, surrealist, satirist, mannerist, or the next Benjamin Britten, serve to narrow our frame of reference and thus our responses to the music."[110]

Yet musical surrealism is an extremely malleable and capacious discursive space, and its elusiveness is the main reason why I think it has served the role that it has in shaping the public image of a composer who prizes instability. Despite the conceptual imprecision of the term, surrealism is a concept that is easy for audiences without extensive musical training to grasp. It is a mental model that requires very little musical background, yet engages an audience member's encounter with an abstract work by asking them to contemplate (if only indirectly) what musical "realism" might be in the first place. It upsets, albeit from an unexpected direction, the idea that new music for the concert hall must also be somehow alienating in its abstraction. Surrealism performs other work as well: it provides a biographical backdrop in the guise of Timothy and Dawn Ades; it creates a means for alluding to "queer" moments in Adès's music, be they specifically sexual or more generally uncanny; it provides a way to discuss Adès's juxtapositions in a way that dodges the ostensible superficiality of postmodern pastiche; it challenges listeners to attend to their own notions of musical norms in order to perceive the nature of Adès's reimagining of them.

These largely extramusical qualities of surrealism might lead some to conclude with resignation that it is little more than a clever way to market Adès's music; Venn seems to note somewhat glumly that public conversations about *Asyla* have tended to settle for what he calls a "music appreciation" approach, which discusses everything except the actual music.[111] Insofar as surrealism reveals Adès's numerous dodges, equivocations, and valorizations of instability, however, it points to a more general *oscillation* on Adès's part, between elements of high modernist aesthetics, and postmodern omnivorousness. I emphasize the word "oscillation" here because it is central to a "metamodernist" view of the present moment across the arts advanced by Timotheus Vermeulen and Robin van den Akker, whom we first encountered in the introduction to this volume.[112] Musical surrealism, distinct from surrealism in other art forms, can achieve this oscillation precisely because it provides a means of ricocheting between an assertion of music's autonomy to the world and concrete points of worldly reference—thus the "sur" and the "realism," as it were. *In Seven Days*—with its hexatonic poles nestled inside a serial process nestled inside a variation form nestled inside a piece of program music—provides just one example of the kind of compositions that can result from such oscillations when Adès refuses to choose a single technical means, rather pursuing numerous ones simultaneously. We can understand Adès's disavowal of the program for *Living Toys* along these lines as well: overspecification made it impossible for the work to oscillate. While this notion of oscillation does not negate John Roeder's idea of multiple temporalities in Adès's work that aligns it with postmodern musical aesthetics, it goes beyond it, reaching into the past in an effort to negotiate what are frequently thought of as mutually incompatible aesthetic strategies.[113] What it boils down to is that surrealism might be "old," but musical surrealism, when considered as a fully articulated discursive paradigm for instrumental music, is as *au courant* as we want it to be. As such, the framework carries out much more cultural work than merely inviting audience members to gamely try to picture melting clocks, deserted piazzas, or fur-covered saucers while they listen to Adès's music.

Hence the rhetoric of surrealism that has swirled around Adès recruits his music into the historical lineage of early twentieth-century modernism while at the same time identifying something new, which is no small feat considering how richly plumbed the consequences of modernism have been. Taruskin's claim that Adès has come "to the rescue of modernism" runs deeper than we might expect for a headline in the Sunday paper. We could also invert Taruskin's comment and note that musical modernism is also helping Adès by allowing him to stand on the shoulders of its giants. Put another way, surrealism provides an aesthetic and historical basis for Adès's prominence today, while being ambiguous enough to leave him plenty of room to maneuver in the future without shedding this marker of canonical belonging. If musical surrealism ultimately survives into the long-term conversation about Adès's music, it is because, in the end, it can be put to so very many purposes. Like Adès's music, it can "slide around on the page," opening interpretive worlds, without slipping off completely.

5

The Great Beyond

There has been a noticeable turn in the sensibility that Adès has brought to his large-scale works since the 2005 Violin Concerto, *Concentric Paths*. During the decade ending in 2016, he gravitated toward grander statements, releasing only three new pieces for smaller ensemble—*The Four Quarters* (string quartet, 2010), *Mazurkas* (piano solo, 2009), and *Lieux Retrouvés* (cello and piano, 2009)—along with a handful of arrangements and reworkings.[1] His larger works from the same period are *Tevot* (2007), *In Seven Days* (2008), *Polaris* (2010), *Totentanz* (2013), and *The Exterminating Angel* (2016). When compared with his output in the 1990s (which comprises more than two dozen works, spanning many different ensemble types, varying in length but clustering under fifteen minutes each in performance), this body of work represents an increased focus on large-scale pieces that require considerable performing forces. Some of this move toward more monumental works reflects Adès's ever-increasing stature in the composition world and the concomitant availability of resources to realize larger visions.[2] At the same time, with greater esteem comes greater independence, and so it is safe to believe that Adès genuinely seeks out these larger-scale forms for their own sake.

Taken together, the five larger works illuminate Adès's increasingly expansive ambition. Consider what preceded the larger works: *Asyla* was intended as something of a floating signifier, *America* was a study in apocalyptic irony, *The Tempest* (as I argue in a previous essay) was an exploration of the ontology of that opera. The Violin Concerto began to hint at a larger preoccupation with the affective qualities of recurring cycles of time, as its subtitle, *Concentric Paths*, indicates. By contrast, Adès's large works from *Tevot* to *The Exterminating Angel* form a series of musical statements that focus on the nature of existence and experience. *Tevot* and *In Seven Days* directly reference biblical themes (Noah's Ark and the Genesis creation myth, respectively); *Polaris* is described as a "Voyage for Orchestra" and bears the name of the most important star in the northern hemisphere for celestial navigation; *Totentanz* sets a medieval dialogue between death and humanity; *The Exterminating Angel* continues to explore aspects of Adès's surrealist affinities but is more fully understood as a sounding of the depths of human

Thomas Adès in Five Essays. Drew Massey, Oxford University Press (2021). © Oxford University Press.
DOI: 10.1093/oso/9780199374960.001.0001.

motivation. The opera's central premise is that a group of guests are unable to leave a dinner party because of some unseen and unknown force; their simple inability to exercise their own agency drives the story forward. In an interview Adès gave on the occasion of the opera's premiere, he dug to the core of his fascination with the plot when he asked rhetorically, "Why do we ever do anything?"[3]

This attention to the cosmic is a surprising turn of events for a man who has been consistently suspicious about metaphysics and grand narratives. At various points throughout his career, although with increasing regularity since 2006, Adès has refused to assign a larger, latent, or hidden meaning to his compositions, despite being given ample opportunity. He disavowed his program for *Living Toys*, claiming that "music should be its own excuse"; he has repeatedly rejected the idea that art serves a "political" function, or that it is "defensible" at all; as noted earlier in this book he told Tom Service that certain material that appears in the Piano Quintet and in *The Tempest* "doesn't mean anything on its own; they're just chords."[4] Rather, Adès typically prefers to focus on the realms of personal aesthetic experience as a central font of meaning. When Service asked him about whether he considered audience members' responses to his music, Adès replied:

> Caring for the time spent listening to one of my pieces has nothing to do with guessing the taste patterns of an audience . . . My work is the only way I can try to understand what it might be like to be in someone else's head. When I'm writing music, I'm partly asking "Is it like this for you?"—but I'm not saying it to a particular person.[5]

While Adès emphasizes subjective experience as an arbiter of musical meaning here, he also remains ruthlessly frank with himself about objective realities. In a different context, when Service asked Adès if writing *Totentanz* had changed his view of his own mortality, Adès merely shrugged: "No, but that is the point: it doesn't matter how I feel about it."[6]

This tension between the subjective and objective qualities of Adès's music forms one basis of my readings here. Scholars and critics of Adès's music have tended to emphasize the objective qualities of his compositions. In the case of scholarly work, this has taken the shape of largely formal discussions about his compositional technique; in criticism it has tended to emphasize Adès's virtuoso command of musical objects and surfaces.[7] One of the consequences of such an approach is that it has tended to neglect the aspects of Adès's music which are transfixing precisely because of the way in which they negotiate subjective and objective musical experience. Although the "subjective" and "objective" will take different forms in each instance, the present essay is a series of close readings of moments in *Tevot, Totentanz*, and *The Exterminating Angel* that bridge this subject–object divide. Despite their heterogeneity as works—an instrumental piece, an orchestral song, and an opera—each of these works carefully balances its subjective and objective dimensions. It is also worth noting that each of these three works features a different primary means of musical signification: *Tevot* operates largely through the use and development of autonomous, "absolute" musical material; *Totentanz* relies heavily on stylistic allusion and the preexisting musical technique of limited aleatory; and *The Exterminating Angel* is a combination of both strategies. Taken as a whole, what emerges from these pieces when viewed in this light is the way in which Adès increasingly uses musical styles and materials to engender subjective experiences which point to truths outside of the objectively observable—his own kind of great beyond.

Tevot

Tevot was Adès's first work for large orchestra without soloists since *Asyla*, which came a full decade earlier. While Adès provided the suggestive title *Tevot*—meaning both "ark" and "barline" in Hebrew—the work lacks any other program or description to guide the listener. *Tevot* is structured as a churning search for a few musical ideas, followed by a prolonged meditation on those ideas. This revelatory process has its precedents. Peter Burkholder highlighted a similar approach as one of the features of several works by Charles Ives, especially the *Concord Sonata*. In that work, the primary theme receives its fullest articulation in the third movement, after extensive development precedes and foreshadows it.[8] In the case of *Tevot*, the revelatory process follows the restless searching and discarding of material that characterizes Ives's sonata. As we will see, this rhetorical hunt for material in the first part of *Tevot* is juxtaposed with a presentation of more straightforward—even "elemental"—material in the second half. This juxtaposition makes a claim on our attention because it shows Adès oscillating between two philosophies of how music achieves a revelatory effect within a single piece.[9]

Adès's own comments about *Tevot* help to motivate such a reading. He has mobilized a veritable army of metaphors to describe the musical processes of *Tevot*, describing *Tevot*'s ending, like that of *Asyla*, as having "an aerial view of the whole thing," which he also likens to pulling "the camera out at the end."[10] In a different context, Tom Service asked Adès about the increasingly "cosmic" quality of his symphonic works since *Tevot*. This time, Adès used the imagery of a spiraling shape:

> I'm aware that, increasingly, my thinking is centrifugal—when you think from a point and everything is spun outwards—rather than centripetal. I recognize this, too, in some symphonists that I really like . . . Sibelius symphonies are fascinating because I think they come from a conflict between the symphonic impulse to bring things round full circle, and an inner desire to go off into an endless horizon of trees or lakes or pure song or whatever it is—the undiscovered country.[11]

In the case of *Tevot* specifically, Adès also described the work in terms of aviation. During an interview from 2007, Adès acknowledged that his thinking about orchestral composition had changed quite a bit in the decade since he wrote *Asyla*:

> When I wrote *Asyla*, I thought that composing music was like tuning a radio. It was as if the music was on the radio, and I could tune my brain in and find it. But now I think it's more like flying a plane—you know you need to land safely, and you need to see all the controls and the whole landscape, and if you get into stormy weather you need to keep hold of everything.[12]

As Adès elaborates this metaphor it seems that the destination is somewhat secondary to overcoming the danger: virtually any flight plan is preferable to a crash. "I would feel that I would absolutely die if I didn't succeed in bringing the piece to harbor."[13]

Each of Adès's analogies here implies that some sort of marked escape from everyday sensory experience is one of the ultimate goals of *Tevot*. In the case of "zooming out," we go from a first-person, human perspective to a bird's-eye view. In the "centrifugal" paradigm, the music metaphorically "flies away" from its center, to some nebulous new terrain—Adès's "undiscovered country." The flight metaphor of Adès's final image is particularly exploratory since it is contrasted with the linearity of simply tuning in to a radio station and (presumably) taking dictation. Each in its own way, these mental models indicate that *Tevot* will reveal to the listener a mysterious object or truth that could not otherwise be known through direct experience. The notion that non-programmatic instrumental music can possess a revelatory purpose traces its origins to the early nineteenth century, and in *Tevot* Adès participates in this practice of music serving as an instrument of revelation.[14] If anything, Adès's turn toward musical revelation in his recent work reflects an engagement with one of the articles of faith of instrumental music: that it is uniquely positioned as an art form to explore the deeper questions of existence. At the same time, the romantics' notion of "inexpressible longing" (E. T. A. Hoffmann's term) in Beethoven has always gone hand in hand with a heroic struggle—the idea that a musical subject will always triumph in the end, though in Ades's case triumph is by no means the inevitable outcome. Instead, Ades's descriptions of sudden changes in perspective in his comments about *Tevot* point the way to understanding a much more nebulous revelation of musical material.

One dimension of *Tevot*'s revelation occurs through the presentation and rejection of musical material in the first part of the piece. As Table 5.1 shows, there are at least five distinct "episodes," which abruptly interrupt the

Table 5.1 *Tevot* Formal Diagram

Structure	Rehearsal	Intrumentation	Notes
Preparation	(beginning of work)	Winds, Strings, Brass	Establish performing force groups as in *Unanswered Question*
	B	Horn	"Unanswered Question" Tune
	F	Oboe	Episode 1: Scherzo
	H	Cello	Episode 2: (Anticipation of BB's fainting movement, but more legato) (*In Volo*, p. 19—sudden rhythmic transformation)
	L		Episode 3: Trumpets
	M	Winds	Episode 4: Fast Scales (Anticipates revelation figure) (Rehearsal O, sudden "tease" theme in oboes) (Rehearsal R, similar to the final question of the flutes)
	S	Horn (solo)	Episode 5: "Rave" p. 41 (reminiscence of L in trumpets) V: another anticipation of the semitone figure
	Y		False Recapitulation (Flutes before Z reveal fakeness)
	Z	Trumpets	"Unanswered Question" Tune
Revelation & Prolongation	AA	Strings	"Revelation"
	BB	Flutes	Descending figure exposition (quasi octatonic approach)
	JJ	Brass	Assertion of pentatonic

existing texture of the work with the presentation of new material. Although a closer look will reveal similarities between some of this material and the second part of the work, on an initial hearing they present themselves as independent sections that interrupt one another and then are just as abruptly discarded. A similar—and highly anthologized—rhetorical strategy is used by Beethoven in the finale of his Ninth Symphony to usher in the "Ode to Joy." In that movement, material from each of the preceding three movements is presented in order, with the cellos metaphorically "rejecting" the existing material, before themselves presenting the "Ode to Joy." In *Tevot*, there is no analogue to Beethoven's cellos to serve as a commentator for the rapid cycling of material, and the material is not a summary of previously encountered music. Nevertheless, the restless presentation of musical material serves a similar rhetorical purpose in *Tevot*, preventing the listener from participating in a continuously unfolding and unified musical experience, instead asking the listener to follow the inquisitive and shifting subjectivity of the work. In both Beethoven and Adès the effect is even further heightened since the second parts of the respective works develop a much more compact set of musical materials, underscoring the ultimately "revelatory" structure of each piece.

Another, more recent, model for the style of organization operating in the first half of *Tevot* is Charles Ives's *The Unanswered Question*. Ives's work (albeit for a smaller ensemble) merits consideration here for the organization of its performing forces and the way that Ives repeats and develops his material. Ives imagined a dramatic role for each instrument family: the strings represent "the silences of the Druids—who know, see, and hear nothing"; the brass (solo trumpet in Ives's case) "intones 'the perennial question of existence'"; the winds carry out "the hunt for 'the invisible answer.'" In *Tevot*, the crackling, amorphous vacuum that opens the work orients the listener in terms of three basic performing forces: the shimmering strings, the gradually descending winds, and the oratorical brass (the percussion, which primarily serves to undergird these other groups, becomes more prominent later). The first extended melodic statement in *Tevot*, at Rehearsal B, comes from a solo horn and echoes the leaping, disjunct arc of Ives's "perennial question of existence." As in Ives's work, Adès uses this tune as a structural marker, for example at rehearsal Z (part of what might be termed the "false recapitulation" in a more conventional structure that begins at rehearsal Y). Similarly, the episodic presentation of material in *Tevot* can also be heard as a "hunt" for meaning in a vein parallel to *The Unanswered Question*. The point here is not so much whether Adès has consciously modeled *Tevot*'s orchestral organization on

Ives's work; rather, it is to point out how the unfolding of *Tevot*—which can seem inscrutable on an initial hearing—can be made legible when viewed alongside other composers' more explicit rhetorical strategies.

The textural parallels between *Tevot* and *The Unanswered Question* reach their apex at AA, which begins *Tevot's* second half. Here, the violins move in a slow, four-part chorus in a high register, texturally inverting the expansive, slow-moving strings that open *The Unanswered Question*. This chorale is a marked departure from the intricately developed material of the first part, and proves to be the background for a simple tune in the winds: the second piccolo presents a simple ascending figure that flirts with an octatonic scale (Example 5.1a). The melodic material remains slow, unfolding as it is taken over by the horns, and juxtaposed with quasi-pentatonic figures by rehearsal HH (Example 5.1b). The rapid presentation and alternation of the first part of *Tevot* is abandoned in favor of an unwavering development of these few musical ideas. In retrospect, we can detect hints of this material in the first half: the descending half steps of the winds at the opening; the fast scales in the winds at rehearsal M. This revelation of material in *Tevot* does not a have a declarative meaning beyond itself, predicated as it is on the use of "pure" musical symbols. Moreover, Adès's closing trumpet figure seems to underscore the provisional nature of whatever is revealed by having the trumpets fall away from C-sharp (a tone in the final chord of A major) to a B (Example 5.2), a tentative backing away that indicates that, whatever truths might reside in the "undiscovered country," they lie beyond the realm of direct perception.

Example 5.1 Adès, *Tevot*, pentatonic and octatonic collections. © 2006 Faber Music Ltd, reproduced by kind permission of the publishers.
a) Piccolo, RBB to RBB+9.

b) Trumpets, RHH to RHH+7.

Example 5.2 Adès, *Tevot*, trumpets, RLL+9 to RLL+13.

When analyzed too closely, such musical revelations can feel anticlimactic; the affective experience of musical time is substituted for the diagnostic language of musical analysis, erasing the rhetorical force of *Tevot* in the process. At the same time, Adès is not the only artist who has posited that laying bare the basic building blocks of a medium can form a pathway to universal truths. Piet Mondrian, for example, justified his abstract paintings on the ground that "there must be a deconstruction of the natural and its reconstruction in accordance with the spiritual."[15] In this light, we can see that Adès in fact recruits two apparently contradictory strategies in his creation of a "centrifugal" work like *Tevot*. On the one hand, we can grasp the rhetorical strategies of rejection and pilgrimage, similar to but not necessarily modeled on those of Beethoven and Ives. Semiotically, we might characterize this as a more "subjective" musical strategy, insofar as it asks us to imagine the music as a persona, performing a quest or journey over the course of the work. On the other hand, in the second half of *Tevot* Adès restricts himself to a bare minimum of musical material, using an "objective" approach of inviting the contemplation of the transcendent qualities immanent in even the most spare musical surfaces.

Tevot is not the only work that Adès wrote that focuses on revelation as an aesthetic goal. His first string quartet, *Arcadiana*, explicitly names imaginary or lost idylls in its movement titles (hewing more closely to a "subjective" strategy of anthropomorphizing the musical material), and a work like *Polaris* can also be seen to gradually reveal its contour according to a non-programmatic logic (recruiting the "objective" qualities of additive melodies to achieve its effect). *Tevot* makes a claim on our attention in this context because of the degree to which it shows a synthesis of these two strategies. Adès's commitment to blending these approaches in *Tevot* provides a conceptual framework for contemplating *Totentanz* as well. In that work, Adès uses material that has readily perceptible references to external genres and styles, juxtaposed against extreme moments of musical objectivity created through limited aleatory, to create a massive statement about the mystery of human mortality.

Totentanz

Totentanz is based on texts from a now-destroyed frieze in Marienkirche in Lubeck, which is structured as a dialogue between Death and representatives from every layer of society, from the pope to an infant. This textual dialogue reflects a musical dialectic between stylistic allusion and a technique championed by Witold Lutosławski (1913–1994) called "limited aleatory."[16] We will see example of these techniques in *Totentanz* shortly; it is important to note first how *Totentanz*'s contrasting impulses reflect Adès's own ambivalence about music's very capacity to engage the subject of death. Given Adès's blunt attitude toward his own mortality, it is unsurprising to find him suspicious of music that is too preoccupied with portraying subjective ecstasy in the afterlife. Redemption in or through music feels problematic for Adès because he perceives that, historically, it has been "more enacted than actually composed."[17] He singled out Mahler's Eighth Symphony as emblematic of the issue: "There's an embarrassment between the job the music's being asked to do and its qualifications for doing that job." Elsewhere, he elaborates: "Mahler's Eighth Symphony particularly is terribly weak. God knows what it's supposed to be about—Jesus, Faust, some nonsense."[18] Yet *Totentanz*, for all of its participation in an artistic genre that reminds the listener of the vanity of worldly pursuits, does not sound the knell of nihilism that Adès found to be the path out of Mahler's dilemma. Rather, in *Totentanz* Adès seems to be asking us to interpret a set of contradictory musical impulses to symbolically represent the ultimately unknowable nature of death.

Adès remarked on music's ability serve as this conduit between everyday experience and transcendent ideals in *Full of Noises*. In that book, he noted that in "a musical work, you can permanently fix something that in life would be appreciable only for a moment. The piece can stand in that relation to one's everyday experience of stability, as an ideally achieved form."[19] With *Totentanz*'s unblinking depiction of death, Adès confronts and prolongs an experience at once fleeting, mysterious, and universal. If anything, *Totentanz* affirms the transcendent capacity of music to illuminate the human condition while remaining ambivalent, through its churning musical switchbacks, about how the subjective contemplation of death is to be reconciled with the blunt reality of its actual experience.

One way to tease this ambivalence from the monumental musical expanse of *Totentanz* is to consider how Adès navigates between subjective and objective signifying strategies over the course of the work. In

Totentanz, we find topical allusions at the subjective end of this spectrum, while Lutosławski's "limited aleatory" fulfills a role as a musically objective technique. Tonality itself serves a synthesizing function in this dialectic, standing as a musical practice that is both musically "rational" and rhetorically forceful. The most evident signifier of all is built into the title of the piece: *Totentanz* is, generically speaking, a dance. In medieval reckonings with death, one purpose of characterizing mankind's relationship with death as a dance is that it was an obvious form of paradigmatic dissonance.[20] If we turn to Adès's musical setting, we not only can detect the presence of dance forms in *Totentanz*; we also find them presented in ways that continue this satirical tradition. The opening piccolo tune, presented immediately after the fanfare, is a lurching descending figure outlining the Dies Irae (Example 5.3). This passage, which is rendered dance-like by its strongly articulated low-brass accompaniment (not shown in the example), hints at isorhythm, yet by varying the rhythm Adès keeps it from settling into such a formal pattern. It constitutes a taunt of sorts which sets the stage for later dance paraphrases in the work. This form of stylistic dissonance is further underscored by the appearance of a lush waltz during the Monk's singing (Example 5.4). The Monk is the second-lowest ranking clergy member featured in the frieze (followed only by *Der Küster* (Parish Clerk)), and the appearance of a loosely constructed Viennese waltz at the end of the section devoted largely to the clerical orders satirically reinforces the vanity of the church hierarchy described in the text. As the work progresses down through the social rungs, the dance references become correspondingly more explicit; hence the emergence of a rustic dance to accompany the appearance of the Peasant (Example 5.5). All of this stylistic allusion drives home the text's core premise, that (to paraphrase Keats) death's dance will eventually be heard by emperor and clown alike. At the same time, by Adès's choice to filter death's omnipresence through an established set of dance idioms, death becomes both familiarized and a subject for aesthetic contemplation. The presentation through dance allows us to walk

Example 5.3 Adès, *Totentanz*, piccolo 2 + 3, mm. 21–31. © 2013 Faber Music Ltd, reproduced by kind permission of the publishers.

Example 5.4 Adès, *Totentanz*, mm. 468–78.

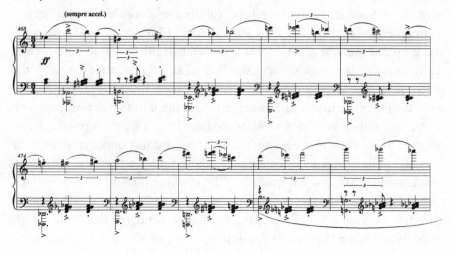

Example 5.5 Adès, *Totentanz*, mm. 755–64.

back from the sheer terror of death and consider it metaphorically in a less daunting manifestation.

If these stylistic references were the extent of Adès's signifying strategy in *Totentanz*, the work would in many ways be a continuation of Adès's love of allusion demonstrated in preceding compositions ranging from *Living Toys* to *Asyla* to *The Tempest*. Yet this rhetorical strategy of referencing dance styles is juxtaposed against the use of musical "objects" in the form of limited aleatory. Limited aleatory is a characteristic process in the later works of Lutosławski. It involves the starting and stopping of concurrent musical cells which are repeated; Lutosławski first used it in his *Jeux vénitiens* (1961). In contrast with more indeterminate practices in the twentieth century, Lutosławski's limited aleatory—also called "aleatoric counterpoint"—fully specifies the pitches and rhythms to be played. It is only the coordination of these individual musical cells that differs between performances. Its presence in *Totentanz* is unusual enough considering Adès's extremely precise and deterministic approach to notating his musical ideas. There is a semiotic role for this limited aleatory as well: given the finality of the topic at hand, Adès's incorporation of this controlled chaos constitutes a surrender of the subjective voice that so strongly characterizes his music. The first climax of the piece, occurring roughly halfway through, is the single best example of this in the work. As the piece hurtles toward this significant catharsis at rehearsal 52, the orchestra is worked into a frenzy, playing an obsessive rhythm but not together: "*independent tempo; uncoordinated; molto rubato, molto appass. accel e. rit. ad lib.*" (Example 5.6). This thunderous climax is followed by a gradual return to conventional notation, although not before a freely notated passage of measured beats, followed immediately by a section where individual strings play short passages independently of one another. Although this section is brief, it is unmistakably distinct from the rest of the surrounding material in its numinous, diffuse quality.

There is an unavoidable interpenetration of these communicative strategies. Adès's decision to include a reference to Lutosławski's aleatory is itself an allusion of sorts—a musical memorial to the commemorated composer. Similarly, stylistic references are objects themselves, insofar as they can be inserted in apparently incongruous musical contexts and retain their integrity as recognizably independent musical ideas. This interpenetration of the subjective and the objective reaches its apotheosis at the end of *Totentanz*, with the arrival of the unambiguous D-major tonality that concludes the piece. Upon the arrival of the duet between Death

Example 5.6 Adès, *Totentanz*, m. 652–55.

Example 5.7 Adès, *Totentanz*, mm. 906–12.

and the child the tonal language becomes radically simplified, and by the final sung word "Tanzen," the harmonic structure is unmistakably settled (Example 5.7). On its own the arrival of D major can be seen as a signifier of stability, or, given the lush orchestration, a nod to the orchestral songs of Mahler—a particularly unexpected allusion given Adès's critiques of Mahler's ability to address such profound questions in his music. In the context of what *Totentanz* is actually asking us to do—imagine the indescribable—the emergence of a stable tonality proffers a synthesis of sorts. One of the longest-running debates in the history of music has been whether music is an objective science of measurement or a more subjective art of persuasion. Various debates about tonality have been the crucible in which those philosophies have been developed. By swerving toward D major so decisively at the end of *Totentanz* (a work which up until then largely avoids common-practice tonality), Adès reminds us that music capaciously contains both the analytical and the rhetorical, even without the use of sophisticated topical allusions or aleatoric objects. Music, he seems to remind us as the last "tanzen" is whispered by the singers, is a singularly powerful instrument in the struggle to understand the extrema of our condition.

The Exterminating Angel

The concluding moments of *Totentanz*, with their repeated "tanzen," present an ambivalent peroration. It points the way to Adès's opera *The Exterminating Angel*, which in its own fashion elevates the contradictions possible through sheer repetition to the status of structural pillar and foundational element of the work's aesthetic force. For Luis Buñuel, the filmmaker who created the movie on which the opera is based, repetition was one of the mysteriously absorbing qualities of the plot of *The Exterminating Angel*. In his comparatively short discussion of the genesis of the film in his memoirs, he draws particular attention to the film's cyclical nature:

> In life, as in film, I've always been fascinated by repetition. Why certain things tend to repeat themselves over and over again I have no idea, but the phenomenon intrigues me enormously. There are at least a dozen repetitions in *The Exterminating Angel*.[21]

Buñuel even suggests that the film itself enjoys a kind of fixating quality in his own life, noting that it is "one of the rare films I've sat through more than once."[22] Also, despite the film's conspicuously surreal dimensions, Buñuel suggests that its core animating feature is quite apparent. "Basically," Buñuel wrote, "I simply see a group of people who couldn't do what they wanted to do—leave a room. That kind of dilemma, the impossibility of satisfying a simple desire, often occurs in my movies."[23] Put another way, Buñuel juxtaposes repetition with frustrated desire, creating a pair of dramaturgical axes. Given the characters' lack of inner drive (which we would typically look to as a catalyst for the plot), Buñuel invites us to conceptualize the film's unfolding desperation by attending to its repetitions.

Example 5.8 Adès, *Exterminating Angel*, Act 1, Prologue, mm. 1–8. © 2015 Faber Music Ltd, reproduced by kind permission of the publishers.

Buñuel's account lights the way for a reading of Adès's opera, insofar as the opera not only follows and elaborates the repetitive strategies found in Buñuel's film, but also relies on a combination of tonal and allusive markers to reflect the unfolding of the characters' "aboulia" (or lack of will) and their efforts to overcome it.[24] The beginning and ending of the opera, in particular, provide musical images that imply a seemingly never-ending story. The opera does not a have a clear opening (Example 5.8); instead we hear a chromatically expanding wedge of bells, played in a slowly mutating rhythm, as the orchestra tunes and the conductor enters. The exchange between Julio and Lucas stops the performance of the bells, but the sonic world of the opera is already in motion. This stepwise movement of the bells returns at rehearsal 80 of the third

act, becoming a freely notated tintinnabulation over the emergence of the text
"libera de morte aeterna et lux aeterna"—paralleling the arrival of the dinner
guests at church at the end of the film version. In an unusual case of strict repetition in the opera, the work ends with eight repetitions of "aeterna," over a
growing crescendo. The eighth repetition abruptly halts on the second syl-
lable; by cutting the chorus off in midsentence the implication is that the repetition could continue indefinitely (Example 5.9). In the opera, as in the film,
we are left on an ominously enigmatic note, with the sense that the dinner
party guests are trapped once again, that the cycle is somehow repeating; yet
we are without a clear indication of the consequences. At this highest level,
repetition provides a structure for the entire work, which is made all the more
unsettling on account of its abrupt termination.

Adès uses a variety of musical techniques to subtly inject other repetitive
elements in *The Exterminating Angel* with structural and semiotic significance. The most obvious repetition, the re-entry of the guests near the beginning of the opera, is perhaps the clearest example. Just as Buñuel's film only
appears to repeat verbatim in the second arrival of the guests—it is actually a
different take, even though the film crew believed it was an editing mistake—
a close look at Adès's repeating material provides one indication of how apparent repetition is actually subtly expressive. In the opera, the tempo is
slowed somewhat in the second repetition and the characters sing at a higher
pitch, as if they are slowly getting caught in a web that dulls their movements
while singing their stress (Example 5.10a and b). Moreover, the conspicuously
"magical" arrival of the word *enchanted* (Example 5.11a,b, and c), relying on
a chromatic mediant relation (from C major to E-flat minor), signals the situational eeriness that the guests inhabit, even if they themselves are not yet
aware of it.[25]

The characters of Eduardo and Beatriz show how Adès relied on tonal signification to increase the expressive effect of repetition. The recurring focus on
the two lovers, and their development over the course of the work, illustrates
how Adès's use of musical material reflects the psychological state (or lack
thereof) of the characters. Eduardo and Beatriz are engaged to be married,
and seem to be the only guests at the dinner who are able to exercise their
wills—through their ultimate suicide in Act 3, Scene 3. In their duet from Act
1 (titled "Berceuse"), we are not told directly what will happen to the couple,
yet vocal lines indicate the impending doom on two accounts. First, Eduardo
and Beatriz sing in an unambiguously tonal context. Eduardo outlines a
B-flat-minor scale, followed immediately by Beatriz doing the same with a
C-minor harmonic collection (Example 5.12a). Insofar as a tonal context
might represent the will, their mutual ability to keep their tonal bearings can

Example 5.9 Adès, *Exterminating Angel*, Act 3, mm. 1051–68.

Example 5.9 *Continued*

Example 5.9 *Continued*

be seen to musically indicate their retaining some semblance of agency despite the spell that has descended upon the party. The descending stepwise motion of Eduardo's vocal line at the end of the duet implies an anticipated lament without a complete reference (Example 5.12b). The berceuse ends in tonal limbo, a series of softly played chords without clear function, suspending the lover's predicament for the moment. The lovers' duet from the second act, beginning in rehearsal 136, continues to use tonal gestures to imply a sense of agency and undergirds it with a sense of indecision by the pileup of interval cycles based on fifths in each of their vocal lines (Example 5.13a–c). Even during this early part of the opera, the lovers seem to be closing in on what must be done, as the duet centers on F minor while Beatriz sings, "There is one way we can be alone." Yet at the moment of the cadence ending the berceuse, Beatriz shifts to a strange deceptive cadence, with a D-flat underneath her vocal line undercutting the F minor cadence from one direction, and the leap from F to A (instead of A-flat) tainting the cadential resolution from a melodic perspective. By the time we encounter the lovers for the final time, in the third scene of the final act, we hear their "love theme" once again—the sequences of chords that rang out at the end of the Act 2 duet (Example 5.14a). The characters now have committed themselves to a full articulation of a chromatically descending figure, set to the text "lose ourselves in the shadows" (Example 5.14b). While we feel Eduardo and Beatriz pulled by the apparently inexorable allure of death in this duet, the tonal language once again suggests a possible separate interpretation of their will with its sudden shift from B-flat minor to D major at rehearsal 32 (Example 5.14c). As discussed in a previous chapter, this tonal arrangement has been described by Richard Cohn as a "hexatonic pole," a chordal progression that has been used in many repertoires to signal a tonal irreconcilability. Even in death, Eduardo

Example 5.10 Adès, *Exterminating Angel*, Entry of The Guests.

a) Act 1, mm. 65–80.

Example 5.10 *Continued*

b) Act 1, mm. 163–73.

and Beatriz are able to sublimate, but not totally resolve, their resistance to the grim trap of the party.

In a parallel vein, Blanca's recurrent piano playing over the course of the opera shows how the use of so-called "phenomenal" music—music that opera

Example 5.11 Adès, *Exterminating Angel*, Act 1, mm. 209–15.

characters actually experience as music—creates a way of using repeated allusive material as a structural marker. The so-called "Blanca Variations" (which have been separately published by Adès) appear in the sixth scene of the first act. Leticia, distraught at the departure of her servants, throws an ashtray through a window while Blanca begins to play. In a moment that could be easily missed in a live performance of the opera, Leticia quotes one of the primary sources of Blanca's variations, "La Vuelta del Marido" (the Return of the Husband). "La Vuelta" is a *romancero* (a type of Sephardic ballad), with origins in Spanish and Greek Jewish communities (Example 5.15). The intertextual resonances are worth lingering on: in the original song, a woman laments the disappearance of her husband as a knight happens upon her. The knight— who is in fact the woman's husband and recognizes her as his wife—asks for

Example 5.12 Adès, *Exterminating Angel*, excepts from Berceuse (Beatriz & Eduardo's Act 1 duet)

a) Act 1, mm. 858–68.

b) Act 1, mm. 896–906.

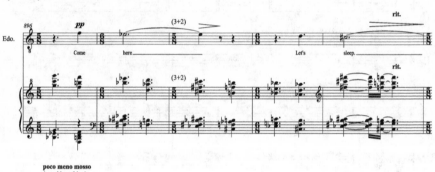

Example 5.13 *Exterminating Angel*, Beatriz & Eduardo's Act 2 duet

a) Act 2, mm. 1660–76.

Example 5.13 *Continued*

b) Act 2, mm. 1683–90.

c) Act 3, mm. 1691–93.

SILVIA comes out of the walk-in cabinet, LETICIA goes in.

a description of the departed love. In the full text of the ballad, the knight subsequently tests his distraught wife's faith. The uncanny quality of the mysterious visitor—a figure who is both known and unknown—easily situates the ballad's premise within the larger sensibility of *The Exterminating Angel*.

In terms of a musical setting, Adès's choice to make Blanca's performance a set of variations on the initial tune that Leticia (and other characters)

Example 5.14 *Exterminating Angel*, Beatriz & Eduardo's Act 3 duet

a) Act 3, "Love" theme, mm. 361–63.

b) Act 3, Descending figure, mm. 372–76.

c) Act 3, Hexatonic pole, mm. 378–82.

Example 5.15 Adès, *Exterminating Angel*, Act 1, mm. 504–16.

sing functions as a musical harbinger of the atrophying of the telos of the characters—of the apparent weakening of their ability to leave. While other forms have more stereotypical arcs in terms of their repetitive structures—sonata form being the most apparent example—a variation form, like a fugue, has no particular obligation except for its own continuation. Although many of the most well-known sets of variations in the repertoire have thunderous finales, they do not necessarily demand resolution in the way that other forms do. In the case of Blanca, her variations end in the first act apparently because they become too difficult for the amateur pianist (the stage directions read that Blanca "plays the piano with extraordinary brilliance," and that "after a particularly difficult passage Blanca stops playing")—the implication being that, were she superhuman, she might very well continue spinning out the variation cycle indefinitely. Indeed, this is one of the defining characteristics of the genre: that they seem as if they can continue forever.

If Blanca seems to have an excess of will in the first act—that it is only physical difficulty that keeps her from continuing—in the second act her solo performance at the piano relies on tonal conventions to indicate an increasing confusion about the direction of her character, and, by extension, of the entire cast. In her piano interlude that begins at rehearsal 113, she seems to

Example 5.16 Adès, *Exterminating Angel*, Act 2, mm. 1374–82.

paraphrase the ascending figure of the variations of Act One, with the inclusion of dreamy trills and an expressive marking that directs Blanca to sing "as if remembering a tune from childhood" (Example 5.16). This time, however, it is Blanca alone who sings, in an imitative (and then inverted) duet with the ondes Martenot in the orchestra. Here, in the place of the gradually developing virtuosity of the variations, Blanca is accompanied by simple block chords, which are largely triads that have been denatured by minor seconds. Such a setting reinforces the aimlessness of Blanca's own vocal line, which slowly orbits the range of various tritones, as if she is hunting for a tonal language but can't find it. The powerful descending minor-second motion she uses on "tell me" further underscores the degraded quality of her will at this point; typically, cadential movement arrives by ascending step from the leading tone to the tonic, not the other way around.

The characters only seem to be freed in the third act with the reemergence of Blanca's variations; by the end of the work it is clear that they are simply trapped in a larger version of the same dilemma. Leticia realizes that the dinner guests must assume the exact positions that they occupied in the first act during Blanca's variation if they ever hope to escape the house, and holds forth with her own enigmatic hymn to freedom (Example 5.17). A listener could be forgiven for missing the spoken invocation of the prophecy from the first act—when the cast sings, almost in passing, that they "will not leave this house until she sings." Yet when she finally accedes to a hymn for the guests, it is an enigmatic paraphrase of Judah Halevi's "Ode to Zion." Halevi was an eleventh-century Spanish Jewish poet, whose writings circulated widely. The ode's rhapsodically ecstatic verse not only fits with the emancipatory moment

Example 5.17 Adès, *Exterminating Angel*, Act 3, mm. 912–31.

of the plot, but also with the broader cabalistic subtext of *The Exterminating Angel* (including, for example, the pair of chicken legs that Leonora carries in her purse, which she explains to Blanca and Leticia are the "keys" that "open the door to the unknown"). Hence Leticia's song, which allows the party to finally leave the house, logically closes the promise made in the first act, yet in such a fantastically esoteric way as to obscure its textual origins. Similarly, the thunderous arrival on D major in m. 1,004, when "The last of the Guests escape" from the house, establishes a powerful tonal resolution, even though D was never a particularly important tonal center for the variations in their original conception. It bears all of the short-term trappings of tonal release with none of the long-term edifice to rationalize it. All of these repetitions at various structural levels through the opera became musical symbols—objects, even—while their subtle transformations indicate the volatile and, with the exception of the lovers, decaying, ability to assert their will or express their inner subjective life.

***

I don't think it was inevitable that Adès's music would assume such a conspicuously philosophical dimension in the decade since *Tevot*. Nevertheless, this trajectory situates Adès's recent large-scale works in the context of a debt to German Romantic ideals of music's sublime potential, while at the same time inflecting those priorities with modernist skepticism, which has a rich intellectual history in and of itself. When Service asked Adès "What are the journeys that your music can take?," Adès replied, "You've stumbled on the finale problem." He elaborated:

> Wagner avoided it, Brahms did it with a weary sense of duty . . . Tchaikovsky is always masterly. Look at the "Pathétique": . . . It's the first one, perhaps, that admits it may all end in doom.[26]

Whatever historical trajectory Adès may be describing here, in this context he seems to suggest that there is a kind of liberation a composer can experience when he or she sees the finale problem for what it is: an opportunity freighted with radical expressive potential.

As for Adès, his approaches to finales in these three works—both musical and existential—situate him once again exactly where we have been finding him time and again: a composer who is recruiting the languages and philosophies of earlier practices as lenses through which to refract the modern world. Adès's steadfast commitment to individual agency in the face of death's ultimate inevitability is perhaps where we find Adès at his most modernist—and, one might note without contradiction, his most transcendent.

This book necessarily ends as Adès's *Exterminating Angel* does: in a midsentence blackout, refusing to even contemplate what might follow. It does not suffer from the finale problem because I knew from the beginning that it would be a fool's errand to seek to say anything conclusive about a composer who has proven to be so dynamic. Yet we might still finish, if not conclude, by noting some of the *ritornelli* in Adès's aesthetic preoccupations. Musical instability is, paradoxically, one of the few constants of Adès's output, so arguably the only real question about the book you now hold is how quickly it will take for the questions I have contemplated here to feel less pressing and be replaced by other churns and eddies. At the same time, his most recent work, insofar as it moves between the allusive and formal strategies in search of larger expressive ambits than any single approach might achieve on its own, underscores a longstanding premise (or promise) of Adès's: to compose in the service of some larger vision—and to keep his output *informelle*. It is hard to picture a future for Adès in which he allows this dialectic to collapse. Works composed after *The Exterminating Angel* (and hence not explored here) suggest this is likely to continue: consider the almost chameleon-like absorption of film scoring in his music for *Colette*, or the frantic, jazz-infused virtuosity of the Piano Concerto. I have but sought to share with you how one contemporary listener of Adès experienced the first two and a half decades of his compositions. Beyond that lies the work of the soothsayer.

Notes

Introduction

1. Thomas Adès and Tom Service, *Thomas Adès: Full of Noises: Conversations with Tom Service* (New York: Farrar, Straus, and Giroux, 2012), 2.
2. Adès and Service, *Full of Noises*, 2.
3. Despite having some clear points of overlap with the synthesis of various strands in *Art Informel* (a term coined by Michel Tapié in the 1950s), Adorno seems more interested in pursuing music on its own terms rather than through comparison with the visual arts.
4. Theodor Adorno, "Vers une musique informelle," in Rodney Livingstone, trans, *Quasi Una Fantasia: Essays on Modern Music* (London: Verso, 1998), 272.
5. Adorno, 306–7.
6. Adès and Service, *Full of Noises*, 122–23.
7. For a full discussion, see Daniel Albright, *Untwisting the Serpent: Modernism in Music, Literature, and Other Arts* (Chicago: University of Chicago Press, 2000).
8. Timotheus Vermeulen and Robin van den Akker, "Notes on Metamodernism," *Journal of Aesthetics & Culture* 2 (2010). DOI: 10.3402/jac.v2i0.5677
9. For a more recent account of the peculiar dilemmas, intersections, and collisions encountered as modernism has moved to the present day, see Seth Brodsky, *From 1989, Or European Music and the Modernist Unconscious* (Berkeley, CA: University of California Press, 2017). "I'm aiming for a certain *inconsistency*," Brodsky writes, ". . . skeptical of a utopian synthesis." (Brodsky, 6. Emphasis in original). See also Tim Rutherford-Johnson, *Music After the Fall: Modern Composition and Culture since 1989* (Berkeley and Los Angeles: University of California Press, 2017).
10. For a discussion of the notion of "structures of feeling," see Raymond Williams, *Marxism and Literature* (Oxford: Oxford University Press, 1977), 128–35.
11. Vermeulen and Van den Akker, "Notes on Metamodernism," 6.
12. Richard Taruskin, "A Surrealist Composer Comes to the Rescue of Modernism," *New York Times*, 5 December 1999, reprinted in Taruskin, *The Danger of Music and other Anti-Utopian Essays* (Berkeley and Los Angeles: University of California Press, 2009), 149; Vermeulen and Van den Akker, "Notes on Metamodernism," 12. Not all commentators see the resurgence of elements of modernism as necessarily indicative of anything besides the wane of postmodernism: "According to the currently accepted periodiziation, the only way to account for a highly visible portion of contemporary practice is to assert that, with the demise of postmodernism, modernism has survived its successor." (Sarah Williams Goldhagen, "Something to Talk About: Modernism, Discourse, Style," *Journal of the Society for Architectural Historians* 64, no. 2 (June 2005), 154). Goldhagen cites Marriane Thormählen's 2003 book *Rethinking Modernism*, which advances a similar argument for modernist literature.

13. Edward Venn, "'Asylum Gained?': Aspects of Meaning in Thomas Adès's *Asyla*," *Music Analysis* 25 nos. 1–2 (March 2006), 115.

14. Warnock has explored how the later canvases of Simon Hantaï perform important work in the history of modernist painting along similar lines, writing, "Hantaï is a key figure for modernity precisely because he brings together two major problematics we tend to think of as distinct—the Surrealist exploration of sexuality and the modernist investigation of medium—and makes them mutually driving for his art." Molly Warnock, "Engendering *Pliage*: Simon Hantaï's *Meuns*," <http://nonsite.org/feature/engendering-pliage-simon-hantais-meuns>, accessed 22 March 2014. At the same time, Hantaï's case also shows that at least one artist negotiated a retrospective gaze toward modernism (he was fascinated with the works of Cézanne and Matisse) with an increasing drive toward abstraction well before the turn of the millennium, nuancing the chronology of the emergence of these oscillating moves that are so central to Vermeulen and Van den Akker's argument.

15. Adès and Service, *Full of Noises*, 75–77.

16. Adès, *Full of Noises*, 83.

Chapter 1

1. Some writing on Adès has already thought about his use of existing materials. Arnold Whittall begins to move in this direction with his discussion of the "pleasures of allusion," rather than the Bloomian "Anxiety of Influence," in his essay "James Dillon, Thomas Adès, and the Pleasures of Allusion," in Peter O'Hagan, ed., *Aspects of British Music of the 1990s* (Burlington, VT: Ashgate, 2003), 3–27. For the most part, however, extended discussions of Adès's music in scholarly journals have tended either toward the synoptic: see Christopher Fox, "Tempestuous Times: The Recent Music of Thomas Adès," *Musical Times* 145, no. 1888 (Fall 2004): 41–56; Elaine Barkin, "About Some Music of Thomas Adès," *Perspectives of New Music* 47, no. 1 (Winter 2009): 165–73; or toward the highly analytical: see Edward Venn, "'Asylum Gained'? Aspects of Meaning in Thomas Adès's *Asyla*," *Music Analysis* 25, nos. 1–2 (2006): 89–120; John Roeder, "Co-operating Continuities in the Music of Thomas Adès," *Music Analysis* 25, nos. 1–2 (2006): 121–54. There are also doctoral dissertations which consider Adès's use of extramusical signifiers, see Nicholas Stevens, "Lulu's Daughters: Portraying the Anti-Heroine in Contemporary Opera, 1993–2013," PhD diss., Case Western Reserve University, 2017; and Emma Gallon, "Narrativities in the Music of Thomas Adès," PhD diss., Lancaster University, 2013.

2. For a discussion of different strategies for conceptualizing intertextuality in instrumental music, see Michael L. Klein, *Intertextuality in Western Art Music* (Bloomington: Indiana University Press, 2005). See also Edward Venn, "Thomas Adès and the Spectres of *Brahms*," *Journal of the Royal Musical Association* 140, no. 1 (2015): 163–212, for a discussion of its resonances in *Brahms*.

3. Liszt's historical legacy lurks behind Adès's glossary in a number of ways. One important difference between Adès and Liszt is that Adès has not had to struggle against a fraught distinction between virtuoso and composer, creating a somewhat different profile for his career than Liszt, who made a conspicuous turn away from the concert stage in 1847. Furthermore, while Adès has not established himself as an improviser as Liszt did, David

Trippett's discussion of the tension between notation and performance in Liszt's oeuvre is recapitulated in Adès's glossary. See Trippett, "*Après une Lecture de Liszt*: Virtuosity and *Werktreue* in the 'Dante' Sonata," *Nineteenth-Century Music* 32, no. 1 (2008): 52–93.

4. Phil Stoecker has also considered the rhythmic invention of the Violin Concerto in "Paths, Spirals, and Extraordinary Cycles: The Chaconne in Thomas Adès's Violin Concerto," paper read at the Annual Meeting of the Society for Music Theory, 10 November 2019.

5. Adès, program note to *Living Toys*. Adès is referencing Stanley Kubrick's film *2001* in this passage, calling the movement in *Living Toys* "H.A.L.'s Death." Adès later suggested that the overall program of *Living Toys* was something of an afterthought. See Adès and Service, *Full of Noises*, 72–74. He is also quick to disavow formalism as an end in itself: "The impulse comes first, the method second. The desire to travel faster preceded the invention of the car. It was desire that generated the design." Adès and Service, *Full of Noises*, 7.

6. The classic statement of this view of translation is given in Walter Benjamin, "The Task of the Translator," translated by James Hynd and E. M. Valk, *Delos* 2 (1968): 76–79. While arrangement is not the same as translation, music scholars have tended to look to theories of translation when musicians change media or notational paradigm. See Jonathan Kregor, *Liszt as Transcriber* (Cambridge: Cambridge University Press, 2010); as well as Margaret Bent, "Editing Early Music: The Dilemma of Translation," *Early Music* 22, no. 3 (August 1994): 373–92.

7. Douglas Hofstadter gives extended treatment to this issue in *Le Ton Beau de Marot: In Praise of the Music of Language* (New York: Basic Books, 1997).

8. Luciano Berio and Rossana Dalmonte, *Two Interviews*, translated and edited by David Osmond-Smith (New York: M. Boyars, 1985), 107. See also Hélène Cao, *Thomas Adès le Voyageur: Devenir Compositeur, Être Musician* (Paris: Editions M.F., 2007), 29–31. Berio also gives this issue consideration in Berio, *Remembering the Future* (Cambridge: Harvard University Press, 2006), 122–41.

9. Adès, note to *Darknesse Visible* (London: Faber Music, 1998).

10. Adès, "performance note," *Darknesse Visible*.

11. Thanks to Ed Venn for pointing this out to me, communication to the author, 25 February 2020.

12. Faber Music, "Thomas Adès, List of Works," <http://works-files.s3.amazonaws.com/9a08f259-0d77-4966-b72b-9a02beeed4f9>, accessed 28 September 2011.

13. Kregor, *Liszt as Transcriber*, 4.

14. Thomas Adès, "'Nothing but Pranks and Puns': Janáček's Solo Piano Music," in Paul Wingfield, ed., *Janáček Studies* (Cambridge: Cambridge University Press, 1999), 18–35. Adès also participated in a conference on British music of the 1990s that took place in 1999 at University of Surrey Roehampton, evidence of a continued involvement with academia. Adès declined to be interviewed for the volume that was an outgrowth of that conference. See Peter O'Hagan, ed., *Aspects of British Music of the 1990s* (Aldershot, UK: Ashgate, 2003), xvii.

15. Adès, "Nothing but Pranks and Puns," 25. For discussion of the Piano Quintet, see Fox, "Tempestuous Times," 47–53.

16. Adès, "'Nothing but Pranks and Puns,'" 21.

17. Adès, "'Nothing but Pranks and Puns,'" 18.

18. Adès, "'Nothing but Pranks and Puns,'" 35.

19. Adès, interview with Andrew McGregor, 20 August 2007, <http://www.bbc.co.uk/radio3/promscomposerportraits/pip/mw2nj/>, accessed 4 October 2011; see also Intermezzo, <http://intermezzo.typepad.com/intermezzo/2007/08/bluebeard.html>, accessed October 4, 2011.

20. Adès and Service, *Full of Noises*, vii.

21. Andrew Porter, "New Sound-Worlds Discovered," *The Guardian*, 18 June 1995.

22. Erica Jeal, Review, *The Guardian*, 27 April 2007.

23. Adès, quoted in Elissa Poole, "Young Composer Lives Up to the Hype," *The Globe and Mail*, 4 May 1998.

24. The visual quality of double orchestras is also reminiscent of Adès's more theatrical use of a clarinetist walking on and off stage in his 1993 work *Catch*.

25. Michael Russ, "Ravel and the Orchestra," in Deborah Mawer, ed., *The Cambridge Companion to Ravel* (Cambridge: Cambridge University Press, 2000), 134–35.

26. Adès and Service, *Full of Noises*, 38.

27. Faber Music, "Thomas Adès, List of Works".

28. "Thomas Adès: New Works for Piano," < http://www.fabermusic.com/news/thomas-ad%C3%A8s-new-works-for-piano-817, accessed 15 December 2018.

29. Other examples of this blurring occur in the "pantomime" in Act I, Scene 2, and the manner in which the Maid's laughter (which opens the opera) anticipates the Duchess's aria in Scene 4.

30. Richard Taruskin has pointed out that manipulation of introversive signing systems can form the basis of a "surrealist" style in an ostensibly autonomous musical work. Taruskin, *The Danger of Music*, 151–52.

31. Eric Drott, "Conlon Nancarrow and the Technological Sublime," *American Music* 22, no. 4 (Winter 2004): 533–63.

32. Thomas Adès, "Like Nothing on Earth: Conlon Nancarrow and the Limits of Aural Amazement," *Times Literary Supplement*, 26 April 1996.

33. Kyle Gann, *The Music of Conlon Nancarrow* (Cambridge: Cambridge University Press, 1995), 86–87.

34. Rolf Hind, email to the author, 8 October 2012.

35. Carolyn Abbate, "Outside Ravel's Tomb," *Journal of the American Musicological Society* 52, no. 3 (Fall, 1999): 465–530; Abbate expands this claim beyond the historical context of the *JAMS* article in "Music—Drastic or Gnostic?," *Critical Inquiry* 30, no. 3 (Spring 2004): 508.

36. In contrast to Abbate, Adès sees virtuosity as an assertion of human subjectivity: "Virtuosity has been suspect for a while—it's said to be just 'for its own sake.' Virtuosity is higher than profundity, or beauty of sound, or giving a touch interpretation of an operatic role . . . Virtuosity pits the individual against failure. Virtuosity is in defiance of our fate, it is a very fundamental thing and if you have it, why would you hide it?" (Adès and Service, *Full of Noises*, 108–9).

37. Kregor, *Liszt as Transcriber*, 183.

38. Adès and Service, *Full of Noises*, 14–16. Adès seems to allow that an excerpt of Wagner might actually have a different effect: "If you take a few slices of fungus or of Wagner, perhaps ten or fifteen minutes, it's magnificent, you can't fault it . . . But when you put it together . . . It seems to me to have a sort of undead quality, a vampiric quality, because he animates these dramas by slices of marvelous music, but they don't build into something real."

39. Taruskin's *New York Times* article on Adès firmly established the surrealist trope as a means of engaging Adès's music with reference to Dawn Ades; see also Fox, "Tempestuous Times"; Cao, *Thomas Adès le Voyageur*; and Stella Ioanna Markou, "A Poetic Synthesis and Theoretical Analysis of Thomas Adès' *Five Eliot Landscapes*," DMA diss., University of Arizona, 2010.
40. Only Thomas adds the accent to the family name, as an aid to pronunciation. See Levy, "Encore for England's Hottest Composer."
41. Timothy Ades, "Comparing You with a Day Possibly in July or August," <http://www.timothyades.co.uk/lipograms.html>, accessed 9 December 2012.
42. Francesca Brittan provides an excellent synopsis of the themes that Kregor raises in Brittan, review of *Liszt as Transcriber*, by Jonathan Kregor, *Journal of the American Musicological Society* 66, no. 1 (Spring 2013), 308–14.
43. Brittan, review of *Liszt as Transcriber*, 308–9.
44. Adès and Service, *Full of Noises*, 48–49.

Chapter 2

1. Norman Lebrecht, "The Arts: The Best of British . . .," *Daily Telegraph*, 23 May 1994.
2. Adès said in one interview "I do slightly worry about pieces, such as the Piano Quintet, that are played a lot because the tunes are nice. I feel they need to be rescued from their own popularity. The noise they make is so attractive that it's hard to hear the music." (Adès, quoted in Brian Hunt, "Aldeburgh's Awkward Guests," *Daily Telegraph*, 27 May 2000.)
3. John Roeder has also explored Adès's use of serial procedures in "Co-operating Continuities in the Music of Thomas Adès," *Music Analysis* 25, nos. 1–2 (March 2006): 121–54; and "Rhythmic Processes in Imitative Post-Tonal Music," paper read at Florida State University, 18 February 2013. Roeder brought to my attention the serialist procedures in the third Mazurka and the second movement of *Lieux Retrouvés*.
4. Other composers have embraced organizing other dimensions of the work, such as duration, serially, moving toward so-called integral serialism. Since Adès's embrace of serialism is primarily focused on pitch, I use it in this less strict sense throughout this chapter.
5. To name just one critique of the problems associated with assigning too much meaning to a composer's intent when it comes to serialism (and therefore allowing a semiotic approach to perform hermeneutic work), see Richard Taruskin, "The Poietic Fallacy," *Musical Times* 145 (2004): 7–34.
6. Arved Ashby, "Schoenberg, Boulez and Twelve-Tone Composition as 'Ideal Type,'" *Journal of the American Musicological Society* 54, no. 3 (Fall 2001): 585–625.
7. Adès, quoted in Peter Culshaw, "'In Seven Days:' Disney's Fantasia—The Sequel," *The Telegraph*, 19 April 2008.
8. For a full-length analysis of the consequences of postwar serialism, see M. J. Grant, *Serial Music, Serial Aesthetics* (Cambridge: Cambridge University Press, 2005). Susan McClary traces the more problematic cultural issues with Babbitt's insistence on absolute musical autonomy from culture—and its concomitant sense of telos—in "Terminal Prestige: The Case of Avant-Garde Music Composition," *Cultural Critique* 12 (Spring 1989): 57–81.

9. Thomas Adès and Tom Service, *Full of Noises* (New York: Farrar, Straus and Giroux, 2012), 99–100.

10. I limit myself to serialism in this chapter because I am interested in exploring its historical valences; in terms of his use of other strict compositional techniques there are several excellent studies of Adès's use of interval cycles. See, for example, Philip Stoecker, "Aligned Cycles in Thomas Adès's Piano Quintet," *Music Analysis* 33, no. 1 (2013), 32–64.

11. Susan McClary states this point of view categorically when she writes, "Back in the days, composers who wanted to gain any foothold in North American and European circles had to—I repeat: *HAD* to—submit to serialism." McClary, "More Pomo than Thou: The Status of Cultural Meanings in Music," *New Formations* 66 (Spring 2009): 29.

12. For an alternative historiography which emphasizes the interpenetration of the arts in modernism, see Daniel Albright, *Untwisting the Serpent: Modernism in Music, Literature, and Other Arts* (Chicago: University of Chicago Press, 2000). Richard Taruskin gives a critique of the teleological fallacies of modernist historiography through his discussion of neoclassicism in his review of Kevin Korsyn's *Towards a New Poetics of Musical Influence* and Joseph Straus's *Remaking the Past* in *Journal of the American Musicological Society* 46, no. 1 (Spring 1993): 124–25. In a different context, Straus challenged what he called the "myth of serial 'tyranny'" by arguing that, statistically speaking, serialism never held sway in musical life in the United States after the Second World War (Straus, "The Myth of Serial 'Tyranny' in the 1950s and 1960s," *Musical Quarterly* 83, no. 3 (Fall 1999): 301–43). Even Straus had to allow that statistics "cannot measure prestige," and it is in terms of the cultural capital of serialism, rather than its statistical significance as a percentage of all musical activity, that I consider the practice.

13. Adorno, quoted and translated in Richard Toop, "Are you *Sure* You Can't Hear It?: Some Informal Reflections on Simple Information and Listening," in Arved Ashby, ed., *The Pleasure of Modernist Music* (Rochester: University of Rochester Press, 2004), 224.

14. Schoenberg, *Arnold Schoenberg Letters*, ed. Erwin Stein, trans. Eithne Wilkins and Ernst Kaiser (Berkeley and Los Angeles: University of California Press, 1987), 164. See discussion in Joseph Auner, "Composing on Stage: Schoenberg and the Creative Process as Public Performance," *Nineteenth-Century Music* 29, no. 1 (Summer 2005): 66.

15. One of the classic challenges to "structural listening" was provided in Rose Rosengard Subotnik, *Developing Variations: Style and Ideology in Classical Music* (Minneapolis: University of Minnesota Press, 1991); additional consideration of Subotnik's ideas were given in Andrew Dell'Antonio, ed., *Beyond Structural Listening? Postmodern Modes of Hearing* (Berkeley and Los Angeles: University of California Press, 2004). Martin Scherzinger's essay the "Return of the Aesthetic: Music Formalism and Its Place in Political Critique" and Joseph Dubiel's "Uncertainty, Disorientation, and Loss as Responses to Musical Structure" from *Beyond Structural Listening* confront this issue of salience particularly directly.

16. Arved Ashby, "The Lyric Suite and Berg's Twelve-Tone Duality," *Journal of Musicology* 25, no. 2 (Spring 2008): 183–210.

17. Anne Shreffler, "'Mein Weg geht jetzt vorüber': The Vocal Origins of Webern's Twelve-Tone Composition," *Journal of the American Musicological Society* 47, no. 2 (Summer 1994): 280.

18. Although Adès theatrically declared that he would "normally" take material that he finds "unnecessary" and "burn it in the sink" (*Full of Noises*, 149), he does in fact retain the majority of his paper sketches and notes (Adès, email to the author, 2 February 2020).
19. Adès and Service, *Full of Noises*, 97.
20. Alexander Goehr, quoted in Arnold Whittall, *Serialism* (Cambridge: Cambridge University Press, 2008), 228.
21. Adès and Service, *Full of Noises*, 151.
22. Adès and Service, *Full of Noises*, 136.
23. Adès and Service, *Full of Noises*, 122–23.
24. A survey of more than 1,200 newspaper, magazine, and scholarly articles written since 1993 mentioning Adès have also failed to yield any direct mention by Adès of Davies or Goehr. In private conversations, Adès has emphasized the influence of Erika Fox, his early composition teacher at junior Guildhall, in contrast to the more academic environment fostered at Cambridge. Adès, email to the author, 2 February 2020.
25. For a full discussion of these two examples, see Whittall, *Serialism*, 224–27.
26. For an overview of Britain's tightly knit networks of concert composition, see Stephen Banfield and Ian Russell's discussion of the conservatory training system in England in their article in Grove. Banfield and Russell, "England (i)," *Oxford Music Online*, https://doi.org/10.1093/gmo/9781561592630.article.40044, accessed 1 January 2019. Harold Bloom's widely cited theory of influence pivots on this idea of "great" poets engaged in a Freudian struggle with those who have come before them. See Harold Bloom, *The Anxiety of Influence: A Theory of Poetry* (New York and Oxford: Oxford University Press, 1973).
27. Adès, quoted in Brett Campbell, "Thomas Adès: Leading Light Composer," *San Francisco Classical Voice*, 22 September 2011.
28. Adès and Service, *Full of Noises*, 3. Several of Adès's works use a low A as a point of stability. "The world is in A Major," he mused in *Full of Noises*, 161.
29. Theodor Adorno, *Philosophy of Modern Music*, translated by Anne G. Mitchell and Wesley V. Blomster (New York and London: Continuum, 2004),115.
30. See, for example, Milton Babbitt, "Who Cares if You Listen? [The Composer as Specialist]," *High Fidelity* 8, no. 2 (February 1958): 38–40, 126–27.
31. Schoenberg criticized Berg for using more than one row simultaneously in the *Lyric Suite*. See Arved Ashby, "Of 'Modell-Typen' and 'Reihenformen': Berg, Schoenberg, F. H. Klein, and the Concept of Row Derivation," *Journal of the American Musicological Society* 48, no. 1 (Spring 1995), 65–105. Muhly wrote of Adès: "He has not written an enormous pile of music, and there's a restraint and a focus to his music . . . that I have yet to discover in myself." (Muhly, "An Alarming Document, Bibimbap, Vibraphone," 13 November 2012, <http://nicomuhly.com>, accessed 4 March 2013).
32. It is also worth noting that this material has affinities with Berg, Adès's apparent preferred composer from the Second Viennese School. This hexachord is also a rather simple derivation of the all interval row, similar to the one Berg used in the first movement of the *Lyric Suite*. See Ashby, "Of 'Modell-Typen,'" 71.
33. Adès and Service, *Full of Noises*, 78.
34. See Roeder, "Co-operating Continuities."
35. Mark Swed, "It's Earnest, Yes, and Funny Too . . .," *Los Angeles Times*, 9 April 2011.

36. "The Importance of Being Earnest—an Opera by Gerald Barry," <http://www.youtube.com/watch?v=gINiIybn6SM >, accessed 28 February 2012.

37. Barry, note to *The Importance of Being Earnest*, Schott Music Shop, < http://www.schott-music.com/shop/products/show,266556,,f.html>, accessed 8 June 2012.

38. Richard Toop, "Are You *Sure* You Can't Hear It?," 224.

39. Liner notes to *In Seven Days* CD and DVD set (Signum Records 277), 2011.

40. Adès and Service, *Full of Noises*, 30–31.

41. Adès and Service, *Full of Noises*, 151.

42. Adès, *In Seven Days* DVD.

43. Adès, *In Seven Days* DVD.

44. Ashby, "Schoenberg, Boulez, and Twelve-tone Composition as 'Ideal Type,'" 587.

45. For a discussion of the "cryptographic sublime," see Abbate, "Music: Drastic or Gnostic?," *Critical Inquiry* 30, no. 3 (Spring 2004), 505–36. The twentieth century's displacement of nature with technology in experiences of the sublime—and Conlon Nancarrow's exemplification of that trend—is described in Eric Drott, "Conlon Nancarrow and the Technological Sublime," *American Music* 22, no. 4 (Winter 2004): 533–63.

46. Schoenberg's metaphysically infused notions of the musical "idea" could also find application in Adès's use of serialism for a biblical story, most obviously in *Moses und Aron*. For one discussion of the fate of Schoenberg's more lofty philosophical ideas for serialism at the hands of later analysts, see Joseph Auner, "Schoenberg's Row Tables: Temporality and The Musical Idea," in *Cambridge Companion to Schoenberg*, edited by Jennifer Shaw and Joseph Auner (Cambridge: Cambridge University Press, 2010), 157–76.

47. Olivier Messiaen, *The Technique of My Musical Language*, trans. John Satterfield (Paris: Alphonse Leduc, 1956), 1:21. See discussion in Richard Taruskin, *Oxford History of Western Music*, vol. 4 (New York: Oxford University Press, 2005), 235.

48. Adès discusses the process of "zooming out" in his comments for the DVD of *In Seven Days*.

49. Adès and Service, *Full of Noises*, 30.

50. Adès and Service, *Full of Noises*, 80–82.

51. Adès and Service, *Full of Noises*, 3.

Chapter 3

1. For the definitive introduction to this aspect of Adès's compositional language, see Edward Venn, *Thomas Adès: Asyla*, Landmarks in Music since 1950 (London: Routledge, 2017). Scott Lee has given consideration to how interval cycles work in *The Tempest* in Scott Lee, "Musical Signification in Thomas Adès's *The Tempest*," PhD diss., Duke University, 2018.

2. Thomas Adès and Tom Service, *Full of Noises* (New York: Farrar, Straus, and Giroux, 2012), 127–28.

3. Barbara Jepson, "'Tempest' Fugit," *Wall Street Journal*, 22 October 2012.

4. Adès and Service, *Full of Noises*, 158–59.

5. "*The Tempest*—A Roundtable Discussion," *The Tempest*, DVD (Deutsche Grammophon, 2012).

6. Brett Campbell, "Thomas Adès: Leading Light Composer," *San Francisco Classical Voice*, 22 September 2011.

7. For a more detailed discussion see William H. L. Godsalve, *Britten's A Midsummer Night's Dream: Making an Opera from Shakespeare's Comedy* (Madison, WI: Fairleigh Dickinson University Press, 1995), 39–97.

8. In this chapter, I follow the convention of the vocal score of Adès's *Tempest*, which uses rehearsal numbers instead of measures.

9. "Tom's Tempest," *The Economist*, 12 February 2004.

10. Zachary Woolfe, "*Mise en Abyme*: Robert Lepage's Concept-Production of Thomas Adès's *Tempest* at the Met Disappoints," *The Observer*, 24 October 2012. For a comparison of Oakes's libretto with other recent efforts, see Andrew Blake, "'Wort oder Ton?' Reading the Libretto in Contemporary Opera," *Contemporary Music Review* 29, no. 2 (April 2010): 187–99.

11. Ariel's gender is fluid in Shakespeare's play: the character self-identifies as male in Act 1 ("to thy strong bidding task Ariel and all his quality"); and is referred to as male in a stage direction but is largely genderless otherwise. In the opera, the role is written for a high soprano. In this essay I follow present convention of respecting self-identification, and use the masculine pronoun throughout to refer to Ariel.

12. In a citational move of his own, Adès nevertheless includes a short fugato in at 2.3.R205, with different text, as Stephano, Trinculo, and Caliban hatch their murder plot.

13. In Shakespeare's play, Prospero does not acknowledge Antonio as he does in Oakes, instead hissing to him in an aside: "For you most wicked sir, whom to call brother would even infect my mouth, I do forgive" (5.1.149–150).

14. W. H. Auden, "The Sea and the Mirror," in Edward Mendelson, ed., *Collected Poems* (New York: Vintage, 1991), 412. Italics in original.

15. Auden, "Sea and the Mirror," 444.

16. Auden, "Sea and the Mirror," 445.

17. In Shakespeare's original, we are certain that Ariel does in fact have at least nominal free will. Yet it remains unexercised, since we learn that he was previously in the service of a witch who trapped him in a tree for disobeying her; presumably Ariel could similarly disobey Prospero but chooses not to.

18. Adès and Service, *Full of Noises*, 11.

19. Ian Bostridge, "Me and My Monster," *The Guardian*, 6 February 2004. https://www.theguardian.com/music/2004/feb/06/classicalmusicandopera, accessed 27 June 2018.

20. Adès and Service, *Full of Noises*, 128.

21. Adès and Service, *Full of Noises*, 159.

22. Adès and Service, *Full of Noises*, 17.

23. Adès and Service, *Full of Noises*, 17. I could—and others do – refuse to take Adès at face value during these pronouncements, since the brilliance of his rhetoric, its perceptiveness and withering authority, come at the expense of some nuance for how he stands in relationship to other composers. I choose instead to read *Full of Noises* for what it is: as a witness of Adès's aesthetic views mid-career, rather than as a work of music history.

24. Adès and Service, *Full of Noises*, 11.

25. Adès, *Full of Noises*, 56–57.

26. For readers familiar with pitch class set theory, these are specifically (027) and (015) pitch-class sets. See discussion in Cao, *Thomas Adès Le Voyageur*, 93.
27. Adès and Service, *Full of Noises*, 48.
28. Hélène Cao, "The Tempest: Thomas Adès," *L'Avant Scène Opéra* no. 222 (2004), 17.
29. Adès, quoted in David Weininger, "At 40, Adès Is Finally at Ease with Attention," *Boston Globe*, 25 March 2011.
30. These features were explored in a pair of papers: John Roeder, "The RICH Logic of Adès's *The Exterminating Angel* and *The Tempest*," and Scott Lee, "Musical Signatures as Dramatic Agents in Thomas Adès's *The Tempest*," both read at "Be Not Afeard: Language, Music, and Cultural Memory in the Operas of Thomas Adès," 24–25 April 2017, London, UK. As Roeder has noted, this gesture also appears in the second movement of *Lieux Retrouvés*.
31. Adès and Service, *Full of Noises*, 28.
32. Adès and Service, *Full of Noises*, 30.
33. Adès and Service, *Full of Noises*, 30–31.
34. Adès and Service, *Full of Noises*, 29.
35. See the discussion in Daniel Albright, *Musicking Shakespeare* (Rochester: University of Rochester Press, 2007), 233–39.
36. Adès and Service, *Full of Noises*, 12.
37. Adès and Service, *Full of Noises*, 13.
38. This count is based on an analysis, by no means claiming to be comprehensive, of more than 300 newspaper articles which compare the two composers either directly or indirectly.
39. Adès, interview with Tom Service at Gulbenkian Foundation, www.youtube.com/watch?v=7lXJ0OS9lgk, accessed 29 February 2012.
40. "We shouldn't worry too much about the so-called 'permanent' value of our occasional music. A lot of it cannot make much sense after its first performance, and it is quite a good thing to please people, even if only for today. That is what we should aim at—pleasing people today as seriously as we can, and letting the future look after itself." Benjamin Britten, *On Receiving the First Aspen Award* (London: Faber and Faber, 1978).
41. Adès, quoted in Barbara Jepson, "'Tempest' Fugit," *Wall Street Journal* 22 October 2012.

Chapter 4

1. Articles about Adès (from both newspapers and academic journals) which mention surrealism include not only Richard Taruskin's *New York Times* article (discussed at length here), but also Timothy Mangan, "From Strauss to Avant-Garde," *Orange County Register*, 19 December 1999; Mark Swed, "Ojai's Two-Nation Summit," *Los Angeles Times*, 5 June 2000; Mark Swed, "Sense and Nonsense at Ojai Festival," *Los Angeles Times*, 6 June 2000; Nadine Meisner, "Pick of the Week," *The Independent*, 24 May 2003; Judith Mackrell, "Invisible Dance in Glasgow," *The Guardian*, 2 June 2003; Mark Swed, "Keep Everyone Guessing," *Los Angeles Times*, 12 February 2004; Anthony Holden, "A Truly Prosperous Prospero," *The Observer*, 15 February 2004; Christopher Fox, "Tempestuous Times: The Recent Music of Thomas Adès, *The Musical Times* 145, no. 1888 (Fall 2004): 41–56; David Gillard, "It was a Dark and Stormy Night . . . ," *Daily Mail*, 16 March 2007; Neil Fisher, "BCMG/Adès," *The Times*, 27 March 2007; Vivien Schweitzer, "Great Expectations, and Versatility to Match,"

New York Times, 23 March 2008; and Tom Service, "A Guide to Thomas Adès's Music," *On Classical Blog*, <http://www.theguardian.com/music/tomserviceblog/2012/oct/01/thomas-ades-contemporary-music-guide>, accessed 31 December 2013.

2. Any number of composers have had individual works or a small cluster of works considered surreal while at the same time not acquiring the marker of a surrealist composer across the entirety of their output. Maurice Ravel (with *L'Enfant et les sortilèges*) and Virgil Thomson (with *Four Saints in Three Acts* and his *Exquisite Corpse* collaborations with John Cage, Henry Cowell, and Lou Harrison) are two such examples.

3. Following other scholars, I use "queer" here as an umbrella term to refer to an array of non-heterosexual subject positions and expressions thereof, mainly in order to allow this essay to embrace one of the main appeals of the term in both academic and popular spheres— its deliberate lack of specificity. For an introductory exposition of the term, its additional resonances, and some of its more important theorizations, see Lloyd Whitesell, "Britten's Dubious Trysts," *Journal of the American Musicological Society* 56, no. 3 (2003): 638n1.

4. See Edward Venn, "'Asylum Gained'? Aspects of Meaning in Thomas Adès *Asyla*," *Music Analysis* 25, nos. 1–2 (March 2006): 89–120; and Kenneth Gloag, "Thomas Adès and the 'Narrative Agendas' of 'Absolute Music,'" in Beate Neumeier, ed., *Dichotonies: Gender and Music* (Heidelberg: Winter Verlag, 2009), 97–110 for discussions of how musical meaning unfolds in Adès's works, especially *Asyla*.

5. Philip Rupprecht has argued that there was a more general "time-lag" trope in British musical historiography in the 1950s, wherein British composers were seen to be "catching up" to established practices on the continent. While Adès's technical means are diverse, one could argue that efforts to understand Adès vis-à-vis surrealism are vestiges of this trend toward framing British composers in terms of earlier debates. Rupprecht, "'Something Slightly Indecent:' British Composers, the European Avant-Garde, and National Stereotypes in the 1950s," *Musical Quarterly* 91 (2009): 275–326, 290ff.

6. Carl Dahlhaus provides a consideration of the durability of, and problems with, the prestige of the new in "'New Music' as Historical Category," in *Schoenberg and the New Music*, translated by Derrick Puffett and Alfred Clayton (Cambridge: Cambridge University Press, 1987), 1–13.

7. Adès, quoted in Schweitzer, "Great Expectations."

8. Breton also celebrated unfettered freedom in creative thought. "The mere word 'freedom' is the only one that still excites me." André Breton, *Manifestoes of Surrealism*, translated by Richard Seaver and Helen R. Lan (Ann Arbor: University of Michigan Press, 1972), 4. See also the corresponding discussion in Raymond Spiteri and Donald LaCoss, eds., *Surrealism, Politics, and Culture* (Burlington, VT: Ashgate, 2003), 6.

9. Adès, quoted in Culshaw, "Don't Call me a Messiah," *The Telegraph*, 1 March 2007. As his book *Full of Noises* amply demonstrates, Adès's preferred method of talking about music is through elaborate and vivid metaphors rather than by means of established analytical paradigms.

10. Thomas Adès and Tom Service, *Full of Noises: Conversations with Tom Service* (New York: Farrar, Straus, and Giroux, 2012), 54.

11. For a discussion of how Adès's "co-operating continuities" form musical effects which place him within one stream of postmodern thought, see John Roeder, "Co-operating Continuities in the Music of Thomas Adès," *Music Analysis* 25, nos. 1–2 (March

2006): 121–54. Of course, postmodernism, like modernism, has meant so many things that no single composer could be expected to address all of its facets. Timotheus Vermeulen and Robin van den Akker propose four main threads in postmodern art and its corresponding discourse: "a transformation in our material landscape; a distrust and consequent desertion of metanarratives; the emergence of late capitalism, the fading of historicism, and the waning of affect; and a new regime in the arts." See Vermeulen and Van den Akker, "Notes on Metamodernism," *Journal of Aesthetics & Culture* 2 (2010): 4.

12. Breton wrote in *Surrealism and Painting* that music was "the most deeply confusing of all forms," and that music is "not destined to strengthen the idea of human greatness. So may night continue to descend upon the orchestra." André Breton, *Surrealism and Painting*, translated by Simon Watson Taylor (New York: Harper & Row, 1972), 1. In "Silence Is Golden," he allowed that there might be a "recasting" of the relationship between poetry and music, but hardly fought against what he saw as poets and visual artists who were generally indifferent to music. Breton, "Silence Is Golden," in *What is Surrealism?*, edited and introduced by Franklin Rosemont (New York: Pathfinder Press, 1978), 265–69.

13. Leon Botstein articulated this problem in an introductory essay to a 1992 concert at Carnegie Hall, which was organized alongside an exhibition of Magritte's work at the Metropolitan Museum of Art. Botstein wrote, "The difficulty, of course, is that music, unlike writing and painting—the most familiar surrealist media, was never constructed on an illusion of realism; on the imitation of nature, strictly considered. Even when musical realism became an accepted notion in the 18th and 19th centuries, it was clearly an artificial convention" (Leon Botstein, *Surrealism and Music?: The Musical World Around René Magritte*, <http://americansymphony.org/surrealism-and-music-the-musical-world-around-rene-magritte/>, accessed 31 December 2013).

14. Daniel Albright limits his discussion almost exclusively to works for the stage in his discussion of surrealism in *Modernism and Music*, considering Milhaud's *Le Boeuf sur le Toit*, Les Six's *Les Mariés de la Tour Eiffel*, Poulenc's *Les Mammelles de Tirésias*, and Hindemith's *Cardillac*. Similarly, Nicolas Slonimsky predominantly focuses on opera, as well, including Hindemith's *Hin und Zurück*, Křenek's *Johnny Spielt Auf*, and Britten's *Turn of the Screw* in his discussion of archetypical musical surrealist works. Daniel Albright, ed., *Modernism and Music: An Anthology of Sources* (Chicago: University of Chicago Press, 2004), 309–11; Nicolas Slonimsky, "Music and Surrealism," *Artforum* 5, no. 1 (September 1966): 80–85. Annette Shandler Levitt put it bluntly in a letter to the *New York Times*: "I am not convinced that music, per se, can even be surreal: lacking representational elements, music cannot create the disjunction that is a requisite of surrealism. There must be a realism before there can be a surrealism." Shandler Levitt, quoted in Taruskin, *The Danger of Music* (Berkeley and Los Angeles: University of California Press, 2009), 151.

15. For explorations of the "automatic" elements which might be read as surreal in different repertoires, see Anne LeBaron, "Reflections of Surrealism in Postmodern Musics," in Joseph Auner and Judith Lochhead, eds., *Postmodern Music / Postmodern Thought* (London and New York: Routledge, 2002), 27–73; Michael Szekely, "Jazz Naked Fire Gesture: Improvisation as Surrealism," *Papers of Surrealism* 9 (Summer 2011), n.p.. Of course, automatism and composition are not necessarily mutually exclusive: in his autobiography, Virgil Thomson described his composition of the first act of *Four Saints in Three*

Acts as a kind of frozen improvisation, where he improvised to Gertrude Stein's libretto until it came in to shape, only then committing it to paper. Virgil Thomson, *Virgil Thomson* (New York: Knopf, 1966), 104.

16. Readers steeped in the history of surrealism will note that I am drawing on a rather narrow and well-known slice of the movement in this discussion. If Adès's music is to be meaningfully interpreted as surrealist for a broad audience, I would argue this is a necessary dimension of its framing. Insofar as surrealism swirls around Adès in the popular press so that it might initiate a listener into his sonic world, I choose to restrict this discussion to texts and works that a casual listener might know.

17. André Breton, *Oeuvres Completes*, ed., Marguerite Bonnet, 2 vols. (Paris: Éditions Gallimard, 1988), 1:328. Translated and quoted in Albright, *Modernism and Music*, 310.

18. Adès and Service, *Full of Noises*, 100.

19. Adès and Service, *Full of Noises*, 13.

20. For an overview of the intersections of surrealism and politics, see Spiteri and LaCoss, *Surrealism, Politics, and Culture*, 1–36; 300–36.

21. Adès, liner notes to *Anthology* (EMI Classics, 2011).

22. For one overview, see Jordana Mendelson, "Of Politics, Postcards and Pornography: Salvador Dalí's *Le Mythe Tragique de l'Angélus de Millet*," in Spiteri and LaCoss, *Surrealism, Politics and Culture*, 174–75.

23. Paul Levy, "An Encore for England's Hottest Composer," *Wall Street Journal*, 9 July 1999. Emphasis added.

24. Patrick O'Connor, "Composer has $200,000 to Spend on Silence," *National Post*, 1 December 1999; Robert Orledge, *Satie the Composer* (Cambridge: Cambridge University Press, 1990), xxxv.

25. Melissa Lesnie, "Thomas Adès: Composing the Impossible," *Limelight Magazine*, 14 April 2013.

26. Although *The Exterminating Angel* may initially appear to loom large in an account of Adès's relationship with surrealism, I argue in the final chapter of this book that this opera is best framed as an engagement with larger questions of meaning and existence that he has been exploring in works such as *Tevot* and *Totentanz*.

27. Richard Taruskin, "A Surrealist Composer Comes to the Rescue of Modernism," *New York Times*, 5 December 1999.

28. Headlines are known to be editorial, but this title was retained without comment when it was reprinted in Taruskin's volume *The Danger of Music*.

29. In retrospect this newspaper article can be seen as something of a dry run for the larger redrawing of the historiography of musical modernism that Taruskin sought to effect in his *Oxford History of Western Music*. See Taruskin, *Oxford History of Western Music*, vol. 4, preface (online edition), <http://www.oxfordmusic.com>, accessed 12 March 2014.

30. Taruskin, "Surrealist Composer." Taruskin wrote a postscript to this essay for *The Danger of Music*.

31. Taruskin, "Surrealist Composer."

32. Timothy Ades, <www.timothyades.co.uk>, accessed 12 December 2013.

33. "Text apart, Adès and director-designer Tom Cairns have between them conjured up a magical island entirely persuasive as Prospero's. From the moment the hieroglyph-strewn curtain rises on Cairns's surreal, primary-coloured, Dalíesque landscape, to brooding

brass and strings that swiftly whip up the requisite storm, one is musically and visually convinced that the spirit of Shakespeare's play is in safe, caring, imaginative hands." Holden, "Truly Prosperous Prospero."

34. Swed, "Keep Everyone Guessing."

35. Ivan Hewett, "He's Brilliant—But Can He Deliver?" *The Telegraph*, 2 February 2004.

36. Fox, "Tempestuous Times," 43.

37. These works include *America: A Prophecy, Living Toys*, and *Asyla*. See Fox, "Tempestuous Times," 42–43; Arnold Whittall, "James Dillon, Thomas Adès, and the Pleasures of Allusion," in Peter O'Hagan, ed., *Aspects of British Music of the 1990s* (Burlington, VT: Ashgate, 2003), 3–28.

38. In *Full of Noises*, Adès puts some distance between himself and his critical reception, using the term "critics" in a generally disparaging way. See Adès and Service, *Full of Noises*, 82, 89, 117, 123, 154.

39. Adès, quoted in Matthew Erikson, "Thomas Adès Takes the Reins," *Los Angeles Times*, 6 March 2011.

40. Francisco Coll, "London Sinfonietta & Francisco Coll," <http://www.youtube.com/watch?v=oIbnRtBpEzU>, accessed 28 February 2012.

41. Mark Swed, "It's Earnest, Yes, and Funny, Too," *Los Angeles Times*, 9 April 2011.

42. Barry, quoted in Barbican Center London, "The Importance of Being Earnest—an Opera by Gerald Barry" <http://www.youtube.com/watch?v=gINiIybn6SM>, accessed 28 February 2012.

43. Speaking of the paired love duets between the characters Gwendolyn and Jack and Algernon and Cecily, Barry alluded to surrealist automata as well:

> GB: So it's as if they were almost cardboard, cutout things, that the same tune is used for both passionate—the same music is used for both passionate outpourings of the two acts. As if passionate outpourings are beside the point, really, and are as surreal as anything else . . .
>
> TA: I mean that's one of the things. I'm sure it's true that the sheer sense with the words that the audience would have laughed themselves silly, I'm sure, but it never really touches the ground, that you're sort of skating on thin ice. They must have somewhere in their subconscious thought "is this ok?" [laughter] There's a feeling of getting away with something but you don't quite know what. (Barry and Adès, quoted in Barbican Center London, "The Importance of Being Earnest – an Opera by Gerald Barry").

44. Albright, *Modernism and Music*, 312.

45. Slonimsky, "Surrealism in Music," and LeBaron, "Reflections of Surrealism," are two of the most thoroughgoing efforts in this direction.

46. See Edward Venn's discussion of the issue of stylistic competence in the third movement of Adès's *Asyla* in Venn, "Thomas Adès's 'Freaky, Funky Rave,'" *Music Analysis* 33, no. 1 (March 2014): 67–69.

47. Put yet another way, I treat surrealism here as a discourse, rather than a style. In such a context, surrealism is a series of debates and conversations (rendered in multiple media), rather than a fixed collection of signifiers. One essay that plumbs the consequences of such a distinction (albeit in architecture, rather than music), is Sarah Williams Goldhagen's "Something to Talk About: Modernism, Discourse, Style," *Journal of the Society for Architectural Historians* 64, no. 2 (Summer 2005): 144–67.

48. Roussel's and Roughton's stories are both discussed and quoted (and in the case of Roussel, translated) in Brotichie and Gooding, *The Book of Surrealist Games* (Boston, Mass.: Shambhala Redstone Editions, 1995), 39–40.

49. Jeanette Baxter, "The Surrealist *Fait Divers*: Uncovering Violent Histories in J.G. Ballard's *Running Wild*," *Papers of Surrealism* 5 (Spring 2007): 1.

50. Baxter, "Surrealist *Fait Divers*," 14n25.

51. Levy, "Encore for England's Hottest Composer."

52. One might contrast Adès's approach here with singspiel or even musical theater, where the sung plane of musical existence is frequently interrupted (or alternately, the spoken plane is interrupted by the song) in order to keep the dramatic action unfolding expediently.

53. Philip Hensher, "Sex, Powder, and Polaroids," *The Guardian*, 28 May 2008.

54. Hensher, "Sex, Powder, and Polaroids."

55. Groover, "Fellatio and Fishing Reels in *Powder Her Face* from Opera Vista," <http://blogs.houstonpress.com/artattack/2011/11/powder_her_face_and_then_some.php>, accessed 30 December 2013.

56. The visual pun is arguably two-fold, insofar as surrealists (and their Dadaist forebears) were known for repurposing found objects in new contexts. Hence the compact-as-bed stage setting echoes both Dali's lobster-as-telephone objects and Duchamp's urinal-as-fountain found sculpture.

57. BAMBill, program note to *Powder Her Face*, February 2013.

58. The "pantomime" in this scene refers to the fact that the actual Duchess of Argyll was referenced in P. G. Wodehouse's alternate version of the lyrics for Cole Porter's song "You're the Top" from *Anything Goes* for British audiences.

59. This staging is borrowed from Almeida's staged version. See Levy, "Encore for England's Hottest Composer." Furthermore, this is only one way that the scene has been "queered" in its staging. While the medium of film allows for this montage, in the New York City Opera production from 2013 the judge reads his verdict while himself receiving oral sex from a clerk.

60. Hensher, "Sex, Powder, and Polaroids." Hensher's use of the plural "books" here suggests he was probably also familiar with Koestenbaum's *Ode to Anna Moffo and Other Poems*, but his discussion suggests he is referring primarily to *The Queen's Throat*, which was published in 1993.

61. Koestenbaum, *The Queen's Throat: Opera, Homosexuality, and the Mystery of Desire* (New York: Da Capo Press, 1993), 45.

62. Koestenbaum, *Queen's Throat*, 126. Koestenbaum could practically be writing about the fellatio scene when he later notes that "as long as singing is considered natural, however, some vocal techniques will be deemed degenerate; and 'degeneration' was the rhetoric used in the nineteenth century to create the 'homosexual' as a pathological identity." Koestenbaum, *Queen's Throat*, 167.

63. The Centre for the Study of Surrealism and its Legacies (of which Dawn Ades is a co-director) undertook a three-year project on surrealism and non-normative sexualities. In 2010, both of Adès's parents participated in a conference at West Dean College titled "Querying Surrealism / Queering Surrealism," offering another thread in the intersections of Adès's own work with that of his parents. If we are to take Taruskin's claim of the impact

of Adès's parents on his own sensibilities at face value, this project indicates that it may be an ongoing conversation between parents and son.

64. Adès, quoted in Culshaw, "Don't Call Me a Messiah." Adès's comments are prescient, since the season after *The Tempest* was produced at the Metropolitan Opera, the company mounted Nico Muhly's *Two Boys*, which revolved around an attack of one boy on another after a lengthy and labyrinthine relationship online. The critical reception was mixed, and writers from *Opera News*, *The New Criterion*, and *The New York Review of Books* all complained that elements of the work were, in their minds, "contrived." F. Paul Driscoll, "Two Boys," *Opera News* <http://www.operanews.com/Opera_News_Magazine/2014/1/Reviews/NEW_YORK_CITY__Two_Boys.html>, accessed 25 March 2014; Eric C. Simpson, "*Two Boys* Premiers at the Met with Much Fanfare but Little Fire," <http://www.newcriterion.com/posts.cfm/-Two-Boys--premieres-at-the-Met-with-much-fanfare--but-little-fire-7282>, accessed 25 March 2014; Geoffrey O'Brien, "Alone in a Room Full of Ghosts," <http://www.nybooks.com/blogs/nyrblog/2013/oct/29/alone-roomful-ghosts/>, accessed 25 March 2014.

65. To name just one example of Brett's interest in the dynamics of labeling, see Brett, "Musicality, Essentialism, and the Closet," in Philip Brett, Gary Thomas, and Elizabeth Wood, eds., *Queering the Pitch: The New Gay and Lesbian Musicology* (New York: Routledge, 1994), 9–26.

66. In the version for double bass and two clarinets, the bass plays these low notes pizzicato, creating a similar effect.

67. See Nicholas Royle's analysis of this trend in his book *The Uncanny* (Manchester: Manchester University Press, 2003), 97.

68. Sigmund Freud, "The 'Uncanny,'" in James Strachey, ed., *An Infantile Neurosis and Other Works* (London: Hogarth, 1955).

69. In Freud's formulation: "If psychoanalytic theory is correct in maintaining that every emotional affect, whatever its quality, is transformed by repression into morbid anxiety, then among such cases of anxiety there must be a class in which the anxiety can be shown to come from something repressed that *recurs*," quoted in Richard Cohn, "Uncanny Resemblances: Tonal Signification in the Freudian Age," *Journal of the American Musicological Society* 57, no. 2 (2004): 287. See also the discussion in Michael Cherlin, "Schoenberg and *Das Unheimliche*: Spectres of Tonality," *Journal of Musicology* 11, no. 3 (Summer 1993): 361.

70. The doubling of apparently unrelated characters in *Powder Her Face* can be distinguished from the more common practice of having a singer reappear in disguise, an operatic strategy with numerous examples, such as Jove appearing as Diana in Cavalli's *La Calisto* and Wotan presenting as the Wanderer in Wagner's *Siegfried*.

71. Whitesell, "Britten's Dubious Trysts," 645. Despite the frequent comparisons of Adès and Britten, I am reluctant to assign much significance to Britten's operas as a historical model here, if only because of Adès's surprisingly voluble rejection of *Turn of the Screw* in *Full of Noises*. One could always speculate that Adès's violent dismissal of Britten's opera as "dilettantish" conceals, in a Bloomian sense, a deeper debt (Adès and Service, *Full of Noises*, 123).

72. Cohn, "Uncanny Resemblances," 290.

73. As Taruskin points out in *The Danger of Music*, music has also struggled against the idea that it "lacks representational elements," an issue that Annette Shandler Levitt raised in her letter to the editor of the *New York Times* following Taruskin's 1999 article.

74. This is a larger problem of intrageneric musical meaning in general, and has been explored by music theorists from a variety of angles. See Kofi Agawu, *Music as Discourse* (Oxford: Oxford University Press, 2009); Robert Hatten, *Interpreting Musical Gestures, Topics, and Tropes: Mozart, Beethoven, Schubert* (Bloomington: Indiana University Press, 2004); Byron Almén, *A Theory of Musical Narrative* (Bloomington: Indiana University Press, 2008).

75. Taruskin, *Danger of Music*, 152.

76. For one overview of this trend, see William Bolcom, "The End of the Mannerist Century," in Arved Ashby, ed., *The Pleasure of Modernist Music* (Rochester: University of Rochester Press, 2004), 46–53.

77. Szymański, quoted in Adrian Thomas, *Polish Music Since Szymanowski* (Cambridge: Cambridge University Press, 2005), 300; Krupowicz, quoted in Anna Granat-Janki, "'Surconventionalism' in the Interpretation of Pawel Szymański and Stanislaw Krupowicz," *Musicology Today* 4 (October–December 2010): 1–14.

78. Edward Venn, "Thomas Adès and the Spectres of *Brahms*," *Journal of the Royal Musical Association* 140, no. 1 (2015): 163–212.

79. Alfred Brendel, *One Finger Too Many* (New York: Random House, 1998), 29.

80. This is only one of the most striking examples from *Brahms*; Venn provides an exhaustive network of reference points between *Brahms* and works by Brahms in his article.

81. Arnold Schoenberg, "Brahms the Progressive," in Leonard Stein, ed., and Leo Black, trans., *Style and Idea* (Berkeley and Los Angeles: University of California Press, 1984), 398–441. See in particular the discussion of thirds (405–07) and the cellular quality of Brahms's motivic development (429–41). Venn also provides a discussion of how Schoenberg's ideas percolated through British compositional circles in the second half of the twentieth century, providing an intellectual lineage for Adès's responses to both Brahms and Schoenberg.

82. Venn also explores at length how *Brahms* engages the notion of the uncanny in music. It is an especially rich example, not only because Brendel's poem is about ghosts, but also because, as Venn demonstrates, so many ghosts—of Brahms, of Schoenberg, of tonality—also loom in Adès's song.

83. Tom Service, program note to Piano Quintet, <http://thomasades.com/compositions/piano_quintet>, accessed 1 January 2014.

84. Fox, "Tempestuous Times," 46–53; Tom Service, "A Guide to Thomas Adès's Music," https://www.theguardian.com/music/tomserviceblog/2012/oct/01/thomas-ades-contemporary-music-guide, accessed 2 January 2019.

85. Philip Stoecker, "Aligned Cycles in Thomas Adès's Piano Quintet," *Music Analysis* 33, no. 1 (March 2014), 32–64.

86. Fox, "Tempestuous Times," 45. John Roeder has made a similar argument about Adès's *Lieux Retrouvés* in a working paper on rhythmic canons in recent music.

87. Fox, "Tempestuous Times," 48.

88. Adès, program note to *Sonata da Caccia*.

89. Venn, "'Asylum Gained'? Aspects of Meaning in Thomas Adès's *Asyla*," 94–98. Venn is drawing on Nicholas Cook's 1998 study *Analysing Musical Multimedia*; my "against the

grain" readings (to borrow Venn's phrase) here are of a somewhat different nature in-sofar as they consider a swath of Adès's output, rather than a single work, as their plane of analysis.

90. For a discussion of how Cohn arrived at this terminology see Cohn, "Uncanny Resemblances," 286n4.
91. Cohn, "Uncanny Resemblances," 289–90.
92. Cohn, "Uncanny Resemblances," 303.
93. Cohn, "Uncanny Resemblances," 307.
94. Cohn, "Uncanny Resemblances," 314–15.
95. In this respect it is similar to Schoenberg's row for the String Trio that Cohn discusses in his article. Also, Cohn's discussion of the precarious balance of hexatonic poles runs in parallel to Adès's more general idea of an "irrationally functional harmony." As Adès explains in *Full of Noises*, even a standard tonic-dominant relationship can be deployed in confounding ways: "Everyone can recognize that there is some mysterious charge of energy that happens when you move from I to V . . . or from V to I, some magnetism that makes it appear that the two harmonies have an internal relationship, that creates the ef-fect of one solving the other. But in fact, once you have realized that this in not necessarily inevitable . . . you can't go back." Adès and Service, *Full of Noises*, 144–45.
96. See the table and examples in Chapter 3 in this volume.
97. "Nothing in music is better known to us, is more familiar and comforting, than major and minor triads . . . The world inevitably contains dissonance, falseness, and illusion; the musical home provides the guarantee of resolution, restoration, reconstitution, recupera-tion." Cohn, "Uncanny Resemblances," 319.
98. Freud, quoted in Cohn, "Uncanny Resemblances," 289.
99. The same could be said of the programmatic element of Schoenberg's *Trio*, which the composer wrote as a "memorial to his own momentary death." Cohn seems willing to allow Schoenberg's program to sit within his "gallery" without comment on this front. Cohn, "Uncanny Resemblances," 299–300.
100. In the interview portion of the *In Seven Days* DVD, Adès notes specifically that the piano represents human subjectivity, which is why it is so prominent in the sixth movement. One might also draw a parallel with Brendel's poem to the ghost of Brahms, frustrated that no one is actually there to see him. As Venn points out at the beginning of his essay on Adès's *Brahms*, "Brahms's nocturnal piano playing is viewed solely as a nuisance that wakes the children and sends the unfortunate instrument out of tune." He spells out the situation even more pointedly somewhat later in his article: "The narrated response in *Brahms* is to ignore the sensation of being observed: the final minutes of the song (bars 76–114) see the unappreciated and forlorn spirit of Brahms depart to increasingly com-plex versions of the omnipresent descending thirds. With no observers willing to give the spectre flesh, the spirit is all that remains." Venn, "Thomas Adès and the Spectres of *Brahms*," 27.
101. Adès, epigram for *Living Toys*.
102. Childhood was also an idealized trope for the surrealists. Spiteri and LaCoss make this point when they write, quoting Breton, "Unlike the child, for whom the imagination 'knows no bounds', in the adult the imagination was 'allowed to be exercised only in strict accordance with the laws of an arbitrary unity.' In this way the imaginative liberty

of childhood was subordinated to the arbitrary authority of culture." Spiteri and LaCoss, *Surrealism, Politics and Culture*, 6.

103. Adès, program note to *Living Toys*, <http://www.hollywoodbowl.com/philpedia/music/living-toys-thomas-ades>, accessed 7 December 2013.

104. Daniel Albright describes Satie's music for *Parade* as a series of sounds which "took up time without seeming to move forward," and Satie himself famously described it as "furniture music." Albright, *Untwisting the Serpent: Modernism in Music, Literature, and Other Arts* (Chicago: University of Chicago Press, 2000), 190–91.

105. For a compendium of surrealist visual and verbal play, see Alastair Brotchie and Gooding, *Book of Surrealist Games*.

106. Adès and Service, *Full of Noises*, 72.

107. Adès and Service, *Full of Noises*, 25.

108. Adès and Service, *Full of Noises*, 132.

109. Taruskin, *The Danger of Music*, 86.

110. Venn, "Thomas Adès," in Agata Kwiecińska, ed., *Nowa Muzyka Brytyjska* (Krakow: Ha!Art, 2009), 182–201. Original English version provided by Venn.

111. Venn, "'Asylum Gained?'," 93–94.

112. Vermeulen and Van den Akker, "Notes on Metamodernism," 6.

113. Roeder, "Co-operating Continuities in the Music of Thomas Adès," 121. Roeder quoted Jonathan Kramer as his point of departure: "The multiplicity of musical time—that music can enable listeners to experience different senses of directionality, different temporal narratives, and/or different rates of motion, all *simultaneously*—is indeed postmodern." Kramer, "Postmodern Concepts of Musical Time," *Indiana Theory Review* 17, no. 2 (1996): 22, quoted in Roeder, 121.

Chapter 5

1. During this period Adès also released seven works that are arrangements or reworkings of existing pieces: *Three Studies from Couperin* (2006), *Dances from Powder Her Face* (2007), *Concert Paraphrase on Powder Her Face* (2009), *Full Fathom Five* (2012), *Come unto these yellow sands* (2012), *Blanca Variations* (2015), and *Lieux Retrouvés* (for cello and small orchestra, 2016).

2. Some of these works—specifically *Tevot, In Seven Days*, and *The Exterminating Angel*—express not only grander ambitions but do so by drawing on specifically Jewish language: the Hebrew title of *Tevot*, the origin story depicted in *In Seven Days*, the kabbalaistic elements of *The Exterminating Angel*. In several conversations I have had with Adès about his ancestry over the last few years, he has mentioned the branch of his family that were prosperous Jewish businesspeople in Alexandria, Egypt. It has not been a focus of this study to discuss Adès's works in terms of his Jewish heritage or to speculate as to what that would mean to him and how it might manifest in his music. Nevertheless, it does bear mention that this expansion of his symphonic language is happening alongside what seems to be his own deepening identification with his Jewish roots.

3. Salzburger Festspiele, program for *The Exterminating Angel*, 22 July–31 August 2016, 51.

4. Thomas Adès and Tom Service, *Full of Noises* (New York: Farrar, Straus, and Giroux, 2012), 30.

5. Adès and, *Full of Noises*, 100.

6. Thomas Adès, *Totentanz*, https://www.youtube.com/watch?v=2G8ySgSayK8, accessed 26 October 2018.

7. See for example Whittall, "James Dillon, Thomas Adès, and the Pleasures of Allusion."

8. See the discussion of "cumulative form" in J. Peter Burkholder, *All Made of Tunes: Charles Ives and the Uses of Musical Borrowing* (New Haven: Yale University Press, 1995).

9. Ed Venn frames an encounter with *Tevot* along similar lines in Venn, "Metaphorical Bodies and Multiple Agencies in *The Tempest*," in Nichola Reyland and Rebecca Thumpston, eds., *Music, Analysis, and The Body: Experiments, Explorations, and Embodiments* (Peeters: Leuven, Paris, and Bristol, CT: 2018), 133–54. Venn asks of *Tevot*: "Who are the subjects within the container, the ark? How are they figured in the music? Is their passage through (musical) space willed, or guided by some external force?" (135).

10. Adès and Service, *Full of Noises*, 44.

11. Adès and Service, *Full of Noises*, 172. The idea of music "spinning" is a well worn image; virtually every undergraduate music theory class will touch on the idea of musical *Fortspinnung* ("Spinning-forth") as a thematic development strategy in baroque music.

12. Adès, quoted in Service, "'Writing Music? It's Like Flying a Plane,'" *The Guardian*, 25 February 2007.

13. Service, "'Writing Music? It's like Flying a Plane.'"

14. The philosophical underpinnings for viewing instrumental music as a means to a spiritual sublime were built largely by Germans in the late eighteenth and early nineteenth centuries. E. T. A. Hoffmann's writings on Beethoven, in particular, have become emblematic of the sudden surge in cultural prestige that instrumental music enjoyed during this period. See E. T. A. Hoffmann, "Beethoven's Instrumental Music," in Oliver Strunk, trans. and ed., *Source Readings in Music History* (New York: W.W. Norton, 1950), 775–81.

15. Mondrian, quoted in Yve-Alain Bois, Joop Josten, Angelica Zander Rudenstine, and Hand Janssen, *Piet Mondrian* (Milan: Leonard Arte, 1994), 317. See discussion in Daniel Albright, ed., *Modernism and Music: An Anthology of Sources* (Chicago: University of Chicago Press, 2004), 202.

16. Lutosławski looms in both *Tevot* and Adès's imagination in several ways. *Tevot*'s two-part structure also has affinities with an approach to form embraced by Lutosławski, who structured works such as his String Quartet (1964) and Second Symphony (1965–67) with an exploratory, episodic first movement and a more teleological second movement (Charles Bodman Rae, "Lutoslawski, Witold," in *Oxford Music Online*, https://doi-org.proxy.binghamton.edu/10.1093/gmo/9781561592630.article.17226, accessed 26 October 2018). Adès has championed Lutosławski's music as a performer, conducting his Cello Concerto in 2013 in Sydney and playing his *Variations on a Theme by Paganini* as well as conducting his Third Symphony in 2018 (Phillip Scott, "Northern Lights," *Limelight Magazine*, 3 May 2013, Boston Symphony Performance Program, https://www.bso.org/Performance/Detail/93152/, accessed 24 September 2018). *Totentanz*, which was commissioned in memory of Lutosławski and of his wife Danuta, continues Adès's admiration of the older composer through compositional means, particularly in Adès's incorporation of limited aleatory, one of Lutosławski's most characteristic techniques.

17. Adès and Service, *Full of Noises*, 22.

18. Adès and Service, *Full of Noises*, 23. In the case of Mahler, there is a way out in Adès's mind: "When he embraces and celebrates the futility of his life and his music, it's much more successful, for me. The Sixth Symphony, *Das Lied von der Erde*, and especially the Ninth Symphony. Because his material suits futility." Adès and Service, *Full of Noises*, 23.

19. Adès and Service, *Full of Noises*, 2.

20. The topical trivialization of a subject by filtering it through a dance form is a common technique in nineteenth-century music—two well-known examples being the self-satire in the finale of Beethoven's Ninth Symphony during the so-called "Turkish" passage, and the similar disintegration of the *idée fixe* in Berlioz's *Symphonie Fantastique* during the final movement, titled "Dream of a Witches' Sabbath," giving the use of dance topics a multilayered historical significance.

21. Luis Buñuel, *My Last Sigh*, trans. Abigail Israel (New York: Vintage Books, 2013), 239.

22. Buñuel, *My Last Sigh*, 239.

23. Buñuel, *My Last Sigh*, 240.

24. See Venn's discussing in Ed Venn, "Thomas Adès's *The Exterminating Angel*," *Tempo* 71 (April 2017), 21–46.

25. Some theorists describe this chord relation as a "double" chromatic mediant, since the chords themselves share no common tones, enhancing the contrast of their juxtaposition.

26. Adès and Service, *Full of Noises*, 42.

Index

Note: Page numbers in *italics* indicate musical examples or illustrations. A *t* following a number indicates a table.